Praise for Celsius 7/7

'Gove does not take prisoners . . . Gove has done us all a service by uncovering the extremist antecedents of the "moderate" Muslim spokesmen feted by the race relations industry and its sympathisers in the BBC'   *Daily Telegraph*

'Well informed and persuasive . . . Gove provides the essential background – the origins of Islamist radicalism from Sayed Qutb to Maududi, the role of the Muslim Brotherhood and its main present-day representatives, the aims of the jihadists'
Times Literary Supplement

'Michael Gove's provocative and convincing book . . . Gove's argument is thorough'   *Observer*

'Michael Gove is one of the rising stars of the British parliamentary Conservative party on account of the exceptional depth and lucidity of his thinking. Almost alone among British politicians, he courageously opposes the ugly anti-Americanism and hatred of Israel which are currently convulsing British society. His new book, *Celsius 7/7*, is a brilliant analysis of Britain's wilful blindness in refusing to grasp the true nature and extent of the Islamist war upon the west and the resulting culture of appeasement which threatens to undermine Britain's special relationship with America. At a time when the hostilities in the Middle East are ratcheting up Britain's state of denial to an unprecedented level of irrationality and prejudice, Gove's urgent wake-up call could not be more timely or prescient'   Melanie Philips

'The political book of the year so far'   *Irish Independent*

Michael Gove is one of Britain's leading writers and thinkers on terrorism and foreign affairs. He has lectured in Britain and Europe on the root causes of terrorism. He was founding chairman of Policy Exchange, Britain's leading right-of-centre think tank, and he is also a founder member of the Henry Jackson Society, an academic body which makes the case for liberal values in foreign policy. He writes regularly for *The Times*, and has been a frequent panellist on BBC Radio 4's *The Moral Maze* and *Newsnight Review*. In 2006 he won the Rising Star Award at the Channel 4 Political Awards. He is Conservative MP for Surrey Heath and lives in Surrey.

Celsius 7/7

MICHAEL GOVE

PHOENIX

A PHOENIX PAPERBACK

First published in Great Britain in 2006
by Weidenfeld & Nicolson
This paperback edition published in 2007
by Phoenix,
an imprint of Orion Books Ltd,
Orion House, 5 Upper St Martin's Lane,
London WC2H 9EA

1 3 5 7 9 10 8 6 4 2

A CIP catalogue record for this book
is available from the British Library.

ISBN 978-0-7538-2195-4

Printed and bound in Great Britain by
Mackays of Chatham plc, Chatham, Kent

The Orion Publishing Group's policy is to use papers that
are natural, renewable and recyclable products and
made from wood grown in sustainable forests. The logging
and manufacturing processes are expected to conform to
the environmental regulations of the country of origin.

www.orionbooks.co.uk

Contents

It's the Ideology, Stupid

Since this book was published there has been a lively debate, among politicians, through the media, in the public square, about the place of Islam in the modern world.

The balance in any liberal society between the claims of faith and the demands of freedom has always required careful negotiation. The growth in the number of Muslims living in the West, as well as the way in which globalization has meant the values of the West impinge on the Muslim world, requires us to proceed with more care than ever.

But in all the debate about how Islam finds its way in the modern world, a crucial distinction is in danger of being lost. This book has sought to make that distinction clear, and underline its importance. The distinction is the difference between Islam, the great historic faith which has brought spiritual nourishment to millions, and Islamism, the specifically twentieth-century ideology which twists the religious impulse into submission to a new totalitarianism.

As the distinguished historian Michael Burleigh has pointed

out, in his masterful book *Sacred Causes*, the history of the last hundred years has been drenched in blood because man's religious impulses have been 'metabolized' into support for political religions – totalitarian ideologies which offer to create a heaven on earth but inevitably descend into hellish violence and oppression.

Islamism poses a challenge to Western values, indeed to universal human values of freedom, dignity and equality, just as potent as past totalitarianisms. And while the Islamists do not have a Wehrmacht ready to roll across the Ardennes, or a Red Army poised to roll across the north German plain, they do advance, just as fascists and communists sought to, through both military pressure and internal subversion. That the military offensive now is driven by insurgents, terrorists and militias alters the nature of the challenge, but no wise statesman can afford to dismiss the threat to our own security from the establishment of Islamist control over nations such as Iraq, Afghanistan or Somalia. The creation of terrorist safe havens, the encouragement offered to allied fighters across the globe, the inevitable ethnic cleansing and terrible violence attendant on Islamist victories, are all, as we know, from Iran to the Sudan, dangers to our future and affronts to our conscience.

But one does not need to travel to the borders of the Arab and Islamic world to see Islamism advance. In the last year there has been a tragic accumulation of new evidence that suggests our response to this challenge is still, at best, muddled and, at worst, so weak as to invite further and yet further assaults.

Just as this book was published in hardback at the end of June 2006, Ayaan Hirsi Ali, the brave Netherlands parliamentarian who had done so much to alert her fellow Dutch citizens to the dangers of Islamism, was compelled to quit Holland. Her immigration status had become a matter of controversy.

But a greater burden the Dutch state had to bear was the cost of keeping Hirsi Ali safe from Islamists who had sworn to take her life. Hirsi Ali's outspoken defence of women's rights and the liberal values of her adopted homeland had led her to be branded an apostate and condemned to death. On leaving Holland, she explained that the only country in which someone like her, who was prepared to challenge the Islamist advance, could now feel secure was America.

Just weeks later, on 10 August, an apparent terrorist conspiracy to blow airliners out of the skies over the British Isles was disrupted at the last moment. Plans were already at an advanced stage of development when the security and intelligence services averted a disaster which could have caused more casualties even than 9/11.

The very next day a coalition of influential British Muslims sent an open letter to the Prime Minister blaming his foreign policy for offering 'ammunition to extremists' and putting British lives 'at increased risk'. The signatories included three Labour MPs, the Muslim Council of Britain and the Muslim Association of Britain. They argued that Mr Blair had to 'change our foreign policy to show the world that we value the lives of civilians wherever they live and whatever their religion. Such a move would make us all safer.'

Twenty-four hours after British nationals had been arrested for plotting the mass murder of their fellow citizens, and the man the Muslim Council of Britain places in the dock is the Prime Minister. While the rest of the country was struggling to come to terms with the enormity of what had been planned the Muslim Association of Britain already knew where the moral culpability lay – with a government arrogant enough to believe in supporting democracy against terror.

For much of the media this letter was not seen, as it should have been, as a morally compromised and intellectually fatuous legitimization of the Islamist agenda but as just another 'embarrassment' for the Prime Minister.

One month later, in September 2006, it was the turn of the Pope to feel the heat. In a lecture he delivered to Regensburg University Benedict XVI quoted the thoughts of a fourteenth-century Byzantine emperor on Islam in the context of a scholarly discussion of faith and reason. He warned his audience that the words he was about to quote were of a 'startling brusqueness', a clear disassociation on his part from the sentiments expressed. The Emperor Paleologus had certainly expressed himself with a directness that, even over the chasm of seven centuries, has the capacity to startle. Rejecting the principle of forced conversion – the spread of Islam by conquest – Paleologus had argued, 'Show me just what Mohammad brought that was new, and there you will find things only evil and inhuman, such as his command to spread by the sword the faith he preached.'

If the Pope himself had been preaching to that text then such brusqueness might have been expected to inspire a strong reaction. But the Pope was only exercising his right – our shared right – to freedom of thought and speech by holding the thoughts of the past up to contemporary scrutiny. But while we might wish freedom of speech, and inquiry, to be a value of universal worth, the Pope found himself on the receiving end of a torrent of vilification, with the Islamists leading the charge.

The Muslim Brotherhood ideologue Yusuf Qaradawi commented, 'We condemn this and we want to know the explanation of this and what is intended by this. We call on the Pope, the pontiff, to apologize to the Islamic nation because he has insulted its religion and Prophet, its faith and Sharia without any justification.' One of Iran's most influential clerics, Ahmad Khatami, asked the Pope to 'fall on his knees in front of a senior Muslim cleric and try to understand Islam'.

The Pope's words inspired more than just vilification. In a

tragic echo of the reaction provoked by the Danish cartoons of
the prophet Mohammad, Benedict's offering of reasoned argument was met by unreasoning violence. In the Palestinian territories Christian churches were fire-bombed by Islamist
groups who said they were protesting against the Pope's
speech. An elderly Italian nun was murdered in Mogadishu,
where she was working at an Austrian-run hospital which
cared for Somali children. In Iraq, the militia group Jaish al-
Mujahideen (Holy Warriors' Army) announced its intention to
'destroy their cross in the heart of Rome . . . and to hit the
Vatican'. One Islamic extremist group kidnapped a priest,
Paulos Iskander. Another Christian priest was beheaded in
Mosul, his kidnappers having demanded his church condemn
Benedict's words.

There is an irony, too bitter for laughter, in a speech which
discussed Islam's relationship with force provoking such a deep
sense of injury in the minds of Islamists that they murder nuns
to protest against the insulting and unjust notion that they are
somehow attached to violence.

The Pope was not the only public figure in the West this past
year to have the words he had spoken twisted by knaves to
make a trap for fools. Labour's former Foreign Secretary Jack
Straw provoked a debate, which certainly lacked nothing in
heat, over the question of the niqab, the full face veil worn by
some Muslim women.

In a measured article for his local newspaper, Straw, now
Leader of the House of Commons, explained the disquiet he
felt when talking to women who wore the full veil during con-
stituency surgeries. Raising his concerns in a tentative fashion,
Straw ventured the thought that the niqab differed materially
from other forms of cultural and religious dress because
it 'could be seen as a visible statement of separation and
difference'.

Straw was roundly abused for stoking Islamophobia,

arrogantly dictating how women should dress and pandering to the prejudice of a white working class whom Labour wished to woo now that the Iraq war had forever estranged it from Muslim affections. The piquancy of all these accusations being directed at the man who brought the Muslim Brotherhood ally Mockbul Ali into the heart of government and who apologized for the offence caused to extremists by Denmark's free press was seldom observed.

While it is impossible to know quite why Straw did raise the question, the reaction to his article once again gave the generality of the British media an opportunity to heroically miss the point. The adoption of the niqab is not so much a mark of Islamic faith as a badge of allegiance towards Islamist politics. Its growing popularity reflects the troubling growth in the attachment to Islamism of a rising generation of British Muslims.

While Islam itself, like all the Abrahamic faiths, considers modesty and restraint a virtue and enjoins on both men and women respect for the sacredness of the sexual act, there is no specific injunction in Islam which requires the adoption of the niqab as an obligation of the faith. But, for Islamists, the veil serves a double purpose. It dramatizes the rejection of Western values, liberalism and feminism particularly, and it marks the wearer apart as one who has become an internal exile. The principle that Muslims should make themselves exiles – al-muhajiroun – from the corrupt and barbaric society in which they are fated currently to live is central to the Islamist programme.

The real debate which the country needed to have, and which the veil debate failed to become, was not about Islam and England but about Islamism and the West. The requirement to tackle that ideology head on, to identify its advocates, challenge their arguments, shed light on their organizational networks, reject their claims and counter their advance across

the globe is the central argument of this book. As a result of
pressure being applied in that direction, not least from the
Daily Mail writer Melanie Phillips in her book *Londonistan*,
and the *New Statesman* political editor Martin Bright in
his Policy Exchange pamphlet 'When Progressives Treat
with Reactionaries', the government has been compelled to
respond. But even among those ministers sensitive to the
argument, the response still gives rise to doubts about the
seriousness with which the whole machinery of the State is
taking the challenge.

The Secretary of State for Communities and Local
Government, Ruth Kelly, has shown an admirable willingness
to wrestle with some of the intellectual challenges posed by
Islamism and in a speech last October reflected some of the
concerns aired in this book. Specifically, she insisted that bodies which received government money should reflect core
British values and she outlined one example of unacceptable
conduct, the boycott of Holocaust Memorial Day, by the
Muslim Council of Britain, referred to in Chapter 8. Ms Kelly
has also opened government's doors to genuinely moderate figures within Britain's Muslim community and has sought to
empower voices for moderation within British Islam through
the creation of the Mosques and Imams National Advisory
Board (MINAB).

But hopeful as these signs are, they also create new causes
for concern. MINAB was set up in close cooperation with the
MCB and is also run in alliance with the flagrantly Islamist
Muslim Association of Britain. The connections between the
MAB and support for extremism are also chronicled in
Chapter 8, but the government seems not be troubled by the
involvement of an organization which offers apologia for ter-
ror in the policing of Britain's mosques.

Indeed, the inattention to the real threat from Islamism is
tragically apparent in the fate of Finsbury Park mosque. The

establishment which once gave Abu Hamza a secure base from which to preach terror and groom killers stands as a symbol of the failed 'covenant of security' by which the British state sought to 'manage' extremists. Hamza is now, at last, behind bars, thanks to American law-enforcement agencies, but the mosque he once exploited was, on his departure, placed in the hands of a fresh group of extremists. And, almost unbelievably, that handover was not just accepted, but blessed by those charged with guaranteeing our security.

The MAB succeeded Abu Hamza and his associates as stewards of the Finsbury Park mosque months ago, and found themselves welcomed in that role by the Metropolitan Police. The MAB spokesman Dr Azzam al-Tamimi, on the record as a supporter of suicide bombing (as reported in Chapter 8), made clear his determination to secure the mosque for his organization, proclaiming, 'For the first few Fridays we will be organizing for our members from across London to come and pray here so that we have a strong majority. We will not tolerate anyone who will seek to abuse the mosque.'

It is not only in its attempts to counter extremism in houses of worship that the machinery of government has proved faulty. The problem of extremist activity on university campuses has been highlighted by many responsible academics, not least Dr Anthony Glees of Brunel University and Professor Tom Gallagher of Bradford University. In response to those and other concerns, the Higher Education minister Bill Rammell appointed an adviser to improve the teaching of Islam in higher education. But the man he chose, Dr Ataullah Siddiqui, is director of the Markfield Institute of Higher Education, an Islamist establishment set up by followers of the teachings of Mawdudi. The Markfield Insititute and its sponsoring body, the Islamic Foundation, are both intimately intertwined with the Pakistani Islamist party Jamaat-i-Islami.

This pattern of proclaiming the need to counter extremism,

and then allowing extremists to drive policy, characterized the government's approach in the aftermath of 7/7 and continues to impede progress today. What makes this pattern of self-deception so tragic is the continuing clarity with which Tony Blair has delineated the challenge we all face. On occasions as varied as his address to News Corporation executives in America last August and his speech on integration in December, Mr Blair has shown a keen appreciation of the problem posed by Islamism rendered all the more striking by the failure of his administration to match his acute rhetoric with appropriate action.

The eclipse of Mr Blair's power, which this mismatch has only underlined, has, of course, been intimately linked with the war in Iraq. For many in his party, and millions more outside, the traumas of that country are crimes for which he is pre-eminently responsible.

That mistakes have been made in Iraq is, as I wrote when this book first appeared, undeniable. Other writers have made it their melancholy task to chronicle what they see as the specific errors at every stage in the campaign. Whatever weight one wishes to attach to each of these errors there is, however, one central strategic miscalculation which overshadows everything.

Almost from the moment that Saddam was toppled the West's leaders have signalled their intention to leave Iraq at the earliest possible opportunity. The strategy for the war itself, masterminded by Donald Rumsfeld, was predicated on a rapid strike of overwhelming force decapitating the Ba'athist regime and then allowing for a quick handover to a new Iraqi government. The number of troops deployed for the invasion reflected Rumsfeld's desire to execute the decapitation and then swiftly depart. The destruction of Saddam's regime was accomplished in a manner, and at a pace, which appeared to vindicate Rumsfeld's narrow calculation. But the failure to commit sufficient forces to make that victory secure has blighted the promise of that liberating moment.

The necessity for a prolonged partnership with the new Iraqi government, the requirement for effective policing and security in the early years of the new government's life, the likelihood that Ba'athist forces would seek to prosecute an insurgent campaign to destabilize the new government and, above all, the risk to that government's future from Islamists, whether sponsored by Tehran, assisted by Syria or emanating from Saudi Arabia, all underlined the need for a military commitment more determined than that originally envisaged.

But Western leaders, having willed the end of tyranny, did not provide the means by which democracy could be securely entrenched. The scale, and vigour, of military force required to provide security was only fitfully provided. And while there have been occasions when Western troops have secured effective military defeats of insurgent forces, from Fallujah to Tal Afar, a willingness to fight the long war necessary has never been effectively demonstrated.

The consequence of a failure to make that commitment has been the rise of Islamist forces like Moqtadr al-Sadr's, which were not contained when they could have been, and have grown in influence by posing as 'guardians' of a Shia population which the coalition and the new Iraqi government should have been protecting more effectively. The failure to provide the force necessary to constrain those militias has been matched by a failure to demonstrate sufficient strength towards Iran, the sponsor of many of those groups, even as its agents were providing the materiel to target British troops.

For many Iraqis the memory of a previous betrayal by the West haunted even the first, hopeful, days of liberation. The experience of 1991, when Western troops delivered a blow to Saddam, opened the door to a better future, but then left Iraqis to their fate, had made many sceptical of the West's new commitment to their nation. That scepticism has only deepened as pressure in the West has grown to wind down the coalition's presence. The perception that the West does not have the will for a prolonged fight against Islamism, that Western nations will, in the end, let down their friends and hearten their enemies, is only fed by the preparations even now being made for departure.

The process of nation-building, or national reconstruction as we are faced with in Iraq, requires humility and patience. We need to be humble enough to recognize that our errors in the past, not least in 1991, have made our task more difficult now. And we need to be patient enough to see through the business of helping a fledgling democracy establish itself, in a region where democracy is so especially valuable because it is so rare.

The demand for an early withdrawal from Iraq not only disheartens those democrats who have done so much to help establish a genuinely free Arab nation, it risks undermining the sacrifices made by the millions of Iraqis who freely voted for a better future. But, perhaps even more tragically, it encourages not just those Islamists who have made Iraq their battlefield, it emboldens all those who rejoice at renewed evidence of the West's weakness.

Those who call for precipitate withdrawal fail to realize that the fall-out from such a scuttle would not be confined to Iraq's borders, just as those who opposed the war in the first place wilfully blind themselves to the consequences for all of us of a defiant tyrant left free to pursue his genocidal ambitions at the heart of the Middle East.

And those who place their faith in solutions devised by foreign policy 'realists', who wish to see an enhanced role for those currently running nations such as Iran, Syria and Saudi Arabia, have singularly failed to appreciate why we got into this mess in the first place.

Against a dedicated ideological challenge, which has been

consistently encouraged by our weakness, no option is more
certain to endanger our future than retreat. And yet, on every
front, that is what the swelling chorus calls for . . .

1

The Rules of the Game
Have Changed

On 14 July 2005 *The Times* published a photograph of a thoughtful young man at work in a Yorkshire classroom. Mohammad Siddique Khan was pictured, purse-lipped and neatly bearded, in the school where he was employed as a teaching mentor. Khan's CV was one of which any parent might be proud. The son of a foundry worker who had emigrated from Pakistan, he was born in Leeds, where he succeeded at school and went on to university. Happily married, a regular worshipper at his local mosque, Khan's work seemed designed to allow others to enjoy the British dream. His professional life was dedicated to helping the children of recent immigrants make the most of the opportunities open to them in the United Kingdom.

That life ended, however, at 8.50 on the morning of 7 July 2005, when Mohammad Siddique Khan detonated an explosive device on the Circle Line train heading west out of

London's Edgware Road Station. Khan and three others, Shehzad Tanweer, Hasib Husain and Jermaine Lindsay, blew themselves up that day in the first successful suicide bombing attack in the British Isles. Fifty-two people were killed and more than 700 injured.

A terrorist attack on London had been predicted for more than three years. Ever since the 9/11 assault on America, Britain's security and intelligence services had been convinced that the capital was vulnerable. An attack was 'inevitable'. But what few Britons had expected, or anticipated, was that a terrorist atrocity would be executed by their own countrymen. Children of the welfare state, subjects of the Crown, citizens of Cool Britannia; Khan, Tanweer, Husain and Lindsay were, in the words of Boris Johnson in the *Daily Telegraph* on 14 July, 'as British as Tizer, and queues, and Y-fronts and the Changing of the Guard'. What could have driven them to kill? And to murder with such indiscriminate ferocity?

These men were not foreign fighters prosecuting a struggle of national liberation against a colonial overlord. They had been born, nurtured and supported by Britain and its institutions. They were not desperately poor and voiceless outsiders, Franz Fanon's 'wretched of the earth', driven to violence because no other option lay open to them to secure justice. They had enjoyed the freedoms and opportunities of the West, held down respected jobs and lived lives of relative comfort. Nor were they psychopaths, or empty nihilists, who found in violence an end in itself. As they themselves made clear, they saw their violence as serving a cause, and a purpose, higher than themselves. Khan himself proclaimed, in a videotape broadcast after his death: 'We are at war and I am a soldier.'

The war in which they enlisted is the conflict of our times, a struggle between liberal values and resurgent totalitarianism. But it is a war in which many, literally, do not believe. The West faces a challenge to its values, culture and freedoms as profound, in its way, as the threat posed by fascism and communism. But the response to that challenge from many in the West is all too often confused, temporizing, weak and compromised. The precise nature of the threat – Islamism – is barely appreciated by many. Those most engaged in combating the threat – specifically the governments of America, Britain and Australia – have to struggle against intellectual currents that make the vital work of self-defence increasingly difficult.

Public discourse in Britain barely touches on the real nature of the Islamist threat, the intellectual underpinnings of Islamist thinking, its hold on the minds of millions, the calculations that underlie Islamist terrorism and the scope of Islamist ambition. Instead, in a curious inversion, the energy that should be devoted to analysing and combating a totalitarian challenge is directed towards campaigning against those who dare to take the threat seriously.

In this book I hope to offer a brief overview of the ideology that animates today's terrorists, for without an understanding of motivation there can be no effective solution. I also want to draw attention to the environment that has given rise to this new totalitarianism. Without efforts to transform the circumstances that create the ground for the terrorists' ideological advance, the steps we take can only ever be ameliorative and temporary rather than fundamental and lasting.

I hope centrally to help explain what we in the West have done wrong. The primary moral responsibility for acts of evil – and any attempt to qualify the word is itself a moral surrender – rests with the authors of that evil. But leaders, and elites, in the West have made a series of decisions in the past that have encouraged and facilitated the forces now in arms against us. The belief that we in the West bear a measure of responsibility for the conflict we now face is widely accepted, but the real mistakes we have made are not those for which we are regularly castigated by our public broadcasters, tenured academics, establishment think tanks and best-selling blowhards. The errors we need to atone for are very different, and the steps to be taken radically divergent from those urged upon us by the loudest and most influential voices in our national conversation.

In particular I want to look at one issue that is considered central to the terrorists' campaign – the fate of Israel – and explain why it is even more crucial to the conflict than many believe – but for reasons most either ignore, deny or pervert.

There is a particular reason why so many of the influential voices shaping our society's response to Islamist terror are urging us down the wrong path. There is a culture of relativism, a failure to display moral clarity, a corruption of thought on both left and right, as well as a strain of Western self-hatred, that combine to weaken, compromise and confuse our national response to a direct totalitarian challenge. Above all, there is still, after the shattering events of 9/11 and 7/7, Madrid and Bali, a widespread reluctance to acknowledge the real scale and nature of the challenge we face.

In the last weeks of 2005, as it emerged that the 7/7 attack was one of ten recently planned terrorist assaults on the British capital, bombs ripped through naval vessels in Algiers; the German government released a Hizbollah killer in exchange for one of its own citizens held hostage by Islamic fundamentalists; France arrested a dozen North African citizens in possession of a kilo of TNT; Spanish authorities broke up an Al Qaeda cell that included two European converts to Islam; and the head of French counter-terrorism operations revealed that a prisoner he was compelled to release had gone on to head a terrorist cell. Not one of these stories featured in the mainstream British media.

Instead, Britain's leading broadcasters and commentators cleared time and space for the latest stage in the escalating campaign against America's counter-terrorism activities. The possibility that terrorists might have been flown across national borders for detention and interrogation was regarded as the principal threat to Western civilization. The activities of murderous ideologues engaged in efforts to destroy that civilization and its citizens were scarcely noted.

If we seek to plot a way forward by reflecting on the complaints amplified in the echo chamber of British broadcasting, or lent spurious weight by the academic and political elites responsible for foreign and security policy in the past, we will only lose our footing and repeat historic errors. The world in which young men who graduate from Leeds Metropolitan University make it their ambition to become mass murderers, and students of town planning from Hamburg University dream of dying with the screams of airline passengers in their ears as they pilot hundreds of tons of molten steel into an office building, is a world we must remake.

2

The War Against the West

The First World War began with the assassination of Franz Ferdinand, the Second with the invasion of Poland, and the Cold War with the Soviet blockade of Berlin. The war that the West now faces, the conflict that has become known as the War on Terror, began in the eyes of many on 11 September 2001 with Al Qaeda's assault on America. But, like the Pearl Harbor attack with which it has been compared, 9/11 did not mark the beginning of this global conflict, but rather its most audacious escalation.

Well before Al Qaeda succeeded in its efforts to bring its war so spectacularly onto American soil, the Islamist assault had been advancing. In the decade before 9/11 Islamist fighters had taken possession of Afghanistan as a base for their global operations, launched a campaign to take control of Algeria, used Sudan as a launchpad for jihad, attacked American embassies in east Africa, and detonated an explosive that killed seventeen sailors on board the American destroyer the USS *Cole* while it lay at anchor off the coast of Yemen.

Prior to that assault, Islamists had planned attacks on other American targets including attempts to sink the USS *Sullivans* in January 2000 and to detonate a bomb in Los Angeles airport in December 1999. Islamist operations against America date back as far as 1993, when the first assault against the World Trade Center was launched. A bomb planted in the car park below the North Tower killed six and injured more than 1,000 others, but the bombers failed in their intention to collapse the Tower.

America was very far from being the only nation to be targeted by Islamist terror. In Jordan, Al Qaeda members laid plans to bomb four targets at the time of the Millennium. They had identified the Radisson Hotel in the capital, Amman, the border between Jordan and Israel; Mount Nebo, a Christian holy site; and a location on the Jordan River where John the Baptist is said to have baptized Jesus. These targets were selected in the hope of maximizing casualties among visiting Western tourists. Western tourists were also the victims of a series of attacks in Egypt. Sixteen Greek citizens were killed in 1996, nine Germans and their Egyptian driver were killed in September 1997, and in November of that year fifty-eight tourists and four Egyptians were massacred near Luxor.

Since the beginning of the Nineties Islamist fighters have also targeted, among other nations, Indonesia, Pakistan, Israel, Qatar, Spain, Russia, Saudi Arabia, Turkey, India, Australia and Kenya. Tourists, businessmen and travellers of almost every nationality have been victims of Islamist atrocities. Attacks have been planned, and terrorist cells established, in Germany, Italy and France as well as the United Kingdom and most of the Arab world. Nations with colonial traditions, and those that have never played the imperial game, countries that are Christian, Muslim or multi-confessional, nations that supported the Iraq war and those that opposed it – all have been visited by the shadow of Islamist violence.

The roots of the current jihadi assault are various, but wherever Islamists strike, whomever they target, and whatever the interpretation placed upon their actions by commentators in the society that has been attacked, they are united in a single campaign by a common ideology. Mohammad Siddique Khan's posthumously broadcast vindication explicitly linked his actions with the campaign prosecuted by Al Qaeda's leaders, Osama bin Laden, Ayman al-Zawahiri and Abu Musab al-Zarqawi. His enlistment as a soldier was driven, he explained, by his religion: 'Islam – obedience to the one true God, Allah, and following the footsteps of the final prophet and messenger Mohammad'.

The terrorists responsible for the Madrid train bombing were, according to Bosnian police, trained in Al Qaeda camps in that country. They were also, according to British intelligence sources, working in cooperation with a Syrian Al Qaeda fighter who, after leading operations in Europe, was believed to have been in Iraq.

Even where no explicit linkage is established between terrorist cells and known Al Qaeda operatives, the operational style, political rhetoric and ideological justification deployed by different Islamist fighters underlines their shared approach. From the Hamas killers in Gaza to Hizbollah terrorists in Lebanon to Islamist fighters across South-East Asia, from Indonesia to the Philippines, there is a common approach: a ruthlessness in the selection of civilian targets reinforced by a willingness to embrace suicide bombing, a belief that Western influence needs to be cleansed from Muslim lands and a desire to see a narrow and highly politicized form of Islam imposed across the Muslim world.

The global, and interconnected, nature of the Islamist terror campaign can be understood only by grappling with the totalitarian ideology that drives jihadist warriors. While they proclaim themselves soldiers for Islam they are not representative of majority Muslim opinion. Far from it. Islamists are a self-conscious vanguard who look down on other Muslims and consider the majority of their co-religionists as sunk in barbarity or error.

Islamism is not Islam in arms; it is a political creed that perverts Islam, just as fascism degraded nationalism and communism betrayed socialism. Its animating spirit is not the pious devotion of the believer who finds in contemplation, charity and prayer both fulfilment and inspiration. Islamism appeals to that part of the human soul that has always been capable of being drawn to revolution, violence and the exaltation of the self through membership of the elect. There are aspects to Islamism that lend it the same appeal that seduced young men into the Red Guards or the Waffen SS, but there are also specific aspects to the ideology that attune it to the discontents and yearnings of young men in our time. Rather than thinking of Islamism as a variant of a great and ancient faith, it is better to view it in the terms defined by the Italian historian of fascism Emilio Gentile, who explained that totalitarianism is:

> An experiment in political domination undertaken by a revolutionary movement that aspires towards a monopoly of power. It seeks the subordination, integration and homogenisation of the governed on the basis of the politicisation of existence interpreted according to the myths and the values of a political religion. [It] aims to shape the individual and the masses through a revolution in order to regenerate the human being and create the new man. The ultimate goal is to create a new civilisation along expansionist lines beyond the nation state.

Islamists believe in the reordering of society to secure total

submission to a narrow, puritan and fundamentalist interpretation of Islam. They are conducting a civil war within the
Islamic world designed to overthrow existing regimes, which
they consider to be unforgivably apostate, and replace them
with a single and unified Muslim state, the restored Caliphate.
Islamists believe that the sanctity and culture of Muslim lands
are menaced and defiled by Western influences, from capitalism to feminism, which have to be eradicated. That cleansing
process must be accomplished by suicidal violence, because, in
the words of Islamism's most influential thinker, Sayyid Qutb,
'the death of those who are killed for the cause of God gives
more impetus to the cause, which continues to thrive on their
blood'.

Nor should the bloodshed stop at Islam's current borders.
Not just because those nations that are unIslamic constitute
dar-al Harb, the House of War, which constantly threatens the
security of the Muslim world. But also because Islamists are
driven by a divine mission to ensure that the whole earth, in
due course, learns to submit to Islamist rule.

The belief that Islam's sovereignty over the whole globe is
necessary and total was powerfully displayed on BBC TV's
Newsnight in February 2006.[1] Anjem Choudray, one of the
leaders of the UK Islamist group al-Ghurabaa, rejected the
suggestion that he might be happier pursuing his fundamentalist approach to religion and politics outside the secular and liberal political culture of the UK. England, he informed the
viewers, 'belongs to Allah'. And in case we failed to measure
just how far short of Allah's, and his, standards, we fell,
Choudray utterly rejected any notion of accommodating his
beliefs and practices to the norms of our democratic society,
arguing: 'If you put me in the jungle, should I behave like an
animal? Of course not.'

Choudray's openness in claiming England for Allah and
condemning current Western mores as bestial may be shocking,

but it should not be surprising. For there is nothing covert or esoteric about the Islamist approach. The scale, scope and ambition of Islamist thinking is not hidden in any secret protocol or encoded in obscure scripture. It is proclaimed, freely and fully, in the speeches and broadcasts of Islamist ideologues from Osama bin Laden to Anjem Choudray, and it is outlined in the extensive texts of the founding ideologues of Islamism.

But there is a wilful blindness among many in the West who refuse to acknowledge the totalitarian nature of the ideology that drives jihadi warriors. Even though the shelves of every Western bookshop sag under the weight of texts that record the cruelties and barbarism inflicted by totalitarianism in the twentieth century, there seems to be a remarkable reluctance to accept that totalitarian thinking could be behind contemporary cruelty and barbarism. Instead Western commentators attribute Islamist violence to specific, discrete grievances such as the presence of American troops on Saudi soil, the failure to establish an Arab Palestinian state, or the material poverty of Arab peoples. In every case the blame for Islamist violence is laid at the door of the West, for failing to deliver 'justice'.

It is a remarkable commentary on the state of analytical thinking in the West that when faced with mass-murderers, who loudly proclaim the ideological basis of their actions and prophesy victory on the basis of Western weakness, Western thinkers respond by denying the ideological motivation of their attackers and instead reflexively blame the West for stoking grievances. The belief that Islamist violence can be explained by these factors is as flawed as the belief in the 1930s that Naziism could be understood as simply a response to the perceived injustices of the Versailles settlement, which could be assuaged by reuniting Sudeten Germans with their Bavarian cousins.

That response, the classic appeasers' temptation, betrays a

profound misunderstanding of the totalitarian mindset. The Nazis were not capable of being satisfied by the reasonable settling of border disputes. They were motivated by a totalitarian dream of a thousand-year Reich, purged of Jewish and Bolshevik influences, in which Aryan manhood could flourish. Their territorial ambitions in the 1930s were not ends in themselves but mechanisms for testing the mettle of their opponents. Hitler's success in realizing his interim territorial goals established, to his own satisfaction, the flabbiness of the West, emboldened him to go further and created a sense of forward momentum that silenced internal opposition.

Jihadists today are not conducting a series of national liberation struggles which, if each were resolved, would lead to peace on earth and good will to all infidels. They are prosecuting a total war in the service of a pitiless ideology. It is only by appreciating that the enemy we face is a seamless totalitarian movement that we can begin to appreciate the scale of the challenge we must confront. While many jihadist acts – from ritual beheadings to the invocation of scripture before battle – may seem to be throwbacks to medievalism, the Islamist belief system is as much a product of modernity as the capitalism, liberalism and feminism that jihadists abhor. It is only by tracing its similarities to, and departures from, other modern totalitarianisms that we can develop an appropriate response.

Islamism is essentially a twentieth-century phenomenon. Like its sibling ideologies, fascism and communism, it offers followers a form of redemption through violence. Like fascism, Islamism envisages the creation of a purified realm purged of toxic outside influences and internal corruption. Like communism, Islamism is not ethnically exclusive: it seeks to enlist new converts through proselytization, political education and military advances. Like both, it reserves a special hatred for the liberal West, for political freedom, the separation of the public and private realms, dissent, sexual tolerance and a belief in the sanctity of individual life. And like both it finds a dark and furious energy in hatred towards the Jewish people.

Communism, fascism and Islamism have all been responses, indeed reactions, to Enlightenment thought. The intellectual roots of communism lie, naturally, in the works of Marx and Engels, but their work grew out of the ferment on the left in the early nineteenth century and the ground laid by thinkers such as Proudhon. Marx and Engels's work, in turn, was developed by their disciples, from Lenin and Ho Chi Minh to Louis Althusser and Che Guevara. Fascism developed out of the racial 'science' of the late nineteenth century, itself a form of perverted Darwinism, the anti-liberal thinking of German critics of the Enlightenment such as Herder and the celebration of violence advanced by Italian Futurists and German ultra-conservatives such as Martin Heidegger, Carl Schmitt and Ernst Jünger.

The thinkers responsible for shaping Islamism as we now know it are the founder of the Muslim Brotherhood, the Egyptian Hassan al-Banna, the Brotherhood's principal theoretician, Sayyid Qutb, and the Pakistani ideologue Abul Ala Mawdudi. Together they exercise a bewitching, and guiding, influence over the ranks of Islamist terrorists conducting the jihad we face today.

It is important to appreciate that Islamism is not the same thing as Islamic fundamentalism. All Islamists are fundamentalists, but not all fundamentalists are Islamists. Fundamentalism is a specifically religious phenomenon, Islamism is also a political programme. It is informed by a view of mankind permeated by traditional, fundamentalist, religious thought, but Islamism is given special force by its co-option of the revolutionary ardour common to other twentieth-century totalitarianisms.

Islam, like other great religions, has gone through cycles of growth, decline, reinterpretation and revival. At various points

Islamic thinkers have drawn believers back to what they argue are the founding principles and fundamental truths of scripture. In the ninth century Ibn Hanbal in Baghdad preached against innovations in Islamic law and thinking, calling the faithful back to traditional interpretations of the Koran. In the late thirteenth and early fourteenth century, Ibn Taymiyya in Damascus led a similar rejection of attempts to update and reinterpret what he considered the essential and flawless truths of aboriginal Islam. And in the eighteenth century Muhammad Ibn Abd Al-Wahhab in Arabia led another campaign to purge Islam of innovations and restore it to the pristine purity of its foundational texts. Each of these movements, like parallel processes in Judaism and Christianity, sought to rescue believers from heresy by re-rooting the faith in its founding truths.

Contemporary Islamism draws inspiration from this puritan strain in Islamic thinking, but it is more than just a form of religious revivalism. It is a specifically political movement that sees the answer to every social, cultural and moral problem in the implementation of a political programme derived from strict Islamic principles and imposed at the point of a sword. Islamism is not a campaign to restore piety through teaching, preaching and encouragement to private devotion. It is a revolutionary attempt to remake society, by argument certainly, but also inevitably by force, in order to secure total submission to a uniquely austere and militaristic divinity.

Islamism emerged as a political movement in reaction to a specific crisis in the history of the Islamic world. Hassan al-Banna (1906–49) founded the Muslim Brotherhood in Egypt in 1929. It emerged in response to the collapse of the Ottoman Empire at the end of the First World War. The Turkish dynasty that had ruled in Constantinople for centuries had become increasingly decadent and enfeebled. Nevertheless, through its existence the principle of the Caliphate had been preserved.

The idea of Islamic unity under fused spiritual and political authority, so dear to traditionalist Muslims, was still just about intact as long as the Ottomans continued.

With the collapse of Ottoman rule, the dissolution of the Caliphate and the aggressively secular modernization of Turkey initiated by Kemal Atatürk, the Islamic world reached a crisis point. What made the crisis worse was the assumption, burnished within Muslim minds, that their faith was destined to triumph over all competitors.

Islam had enjoyed, for much of its history, the intoxicating sense of forward momentum. The youngest of the Abrahamic faiths, its followers could lay claim to a final revelation superior to those enjoyed by Jews and Christians, and a faith considerably more advanced than that of the idol-worshippers of the East. The sense that the Islamic revelation armed its followers with superior virtue was underpinned by the military and political advances they enjoyed. From an isolated beginning in the arid deserts of the Arabian peninsula, Islam's followers succeeded in subduing a vast swathe of the earth, carrying their faith to the furthest reaches of Asia, across the reach of inhabited Africa, into Europe and to the gates of Vienna. The Moghuls of India and, especially, the Ottoman Turks of Constantinople were regional superpowers. Islam's followers succeeded in repulsing Christian attempts to eat into their territories, with the Crusader kingdoms of the Levant surviving for only a generation or two before succumbing to the irresistible force of Muslim arms.

Within the Islamic world, learning advanced, as mathematics, astronomy, philosophy and poetry were celebrated. Christians and Jews lived a tolerated second-class existence as *dhimmis*, able to follow their own, more primitive faiths, but without the rights of citizenship enjoyed by the followers of the Prophet.

Islamic strength, however, was built on brittle foundations.

As a faith spread primarily by territorial conquest rather than intellectual persuasion, its vitality depended on military prowess. Islamic power slowly began to decline as European nations accelerated their development following the Renaissance and Reformation. From the seventeenth century onwards the crescent was eclipsed from the West.

The intellectual development of the West was stimulated by a variety of factors. The emergence of national sovereignty as an organizing principle of statehood in the wake of the Thirty Years War, the rediscovery of humanist learning stimulated by the Renaissance, the economic growth that accompanied the rise of Protestantism and, in due course, the openness, experimentation, individualism and empiricism that the Enlightenment brought, all gave to Europe a political, monetary and military strength that overawed the Islamic world. As the noted scholar of the Middle East Professor Bernard Lewis has explained, the decline of the Islamic world relative to the West provoked agonized concern within Muslim minds.

The Islamic world was held back by, among other factors, the manner in which faith and power were fused in Muslim lands. The Koran was viewed by Islam's traditionalists as the impeccable, unalterable, word of God, which provided man with a guide for every action, a resolution for every dilemma. The laws by which man was ordered were those that had been divinely revealed, and were therefore incapable of amendment. Islamic ambassadors were bewildered by the sight of European parliaments contending over legislation, exchanging ideas and principles as they evolved new laws and ways of governing that facilitated progress. How could man try to make laws when God had already laid them all down?

Islamic nations were crippled, relative to the West, by their institutional inability to adapt politically. The faith that had imbued traditionalist Muslims with conquering fervour also narrowed minds to such an extent that they were closed to innovation. The position of women, minorities, freethinkers and outsiders was so rigidly marginalized that Islamic society became fossilized. Relative decline led, inevitably, to remorseless fall. Throughout the nineteenth century the Ottoman empire, the still just surviving Caliphate, was the sick man of Europe, alternately preyed on and propped up by Western powers.

After the collapse of the Ottoman settlement, and with it the Caliphate, the sense of trauma was profound. And that sense of loss was only magnified by the remaking of the Arab world by Western hands, those that drew lines in the sand, dividing Islamic nations with arbitrary ease and enforcing the establishment of new jurisdictions at the point of a gun. The perceived division of the Middle East between France, Britain and their clients along lines that became known as the Sykes-Picot agreement rankles to this day. Thrones were found for Arab leaders, but the reality of power was unmistakably Western.

Among Muslim thinkers and leaders, differing explanations were sought for the collapse of Islamic power and the humbling of Arab leadership. The success of the West challenged centuries-old assumptions about the superiority of the Islamic faith and the perfection of the Koranic revelation. The stirrings of questioning began, but the most influential voices to emerge were not those arguing for the embrace of liberalism, empiricism and Western-style progress but those who demanded a very different response. For Hassan al-Banna, Sayyid Qutb and Abul Ala Mawdudi, the answer to Islam's crisis was not reform but reaction. And their message has grown in seductive power over the years.

For Hassan al-Banna and his followers in the Muslim Brotherhood the roots of decline lay in the abandonment of a pure and unpolluted Islam. Revival could only come through a return to a society ordered on the basis of the literal, and unalterable, truths of the Koran.

Al-Banna was born in Mahmuddiya, a small town in the Nile Delta, in 1906, the son of a watchmaker who was himself a notably pious Muslim. Al-Banna was an intelligent and religious youth whose studies took him to the Cairo of the 1920s. Egypt was then under effective British control and al-Banna reacted against what he saw as the decadent Western influences that had taken his own people away from the faith of their fathers, weakened their culture and threatened to pollute further their homeland. In 1927 he moved to Ismailiya, the headquarters of the British-run Suez Canal zone, where he took up a position as a teacher. Working at the heart of a community that symbolized the penetration of Western influence within the Muslim world only reinforced al-Banna's determination to bring 'his' people back to the forgotten truths of fundamentalist Islam.

The Brotherhood was established as one of many societies for religious reform and fellowship in 1920s Egypt, but it soon overtook its competitors as the foremost organization of its kind. It offered a home to all those who wished to purge their land of Western influences, put past humiliations behind them, recover their pride, submit to a cause greater than themselves and bring forward a spiritual renaissance in which their nation could emerge purified and exalted. In that respect the Brotherhood emulated the rise of the Nazi Party in Germany at exactly the same time.

Just as the Nazis emerged from a ferment of far-Right and Volkisch groups seeking to regenerate Germany after the so-called humiliation of Versailles, so the Brotherhood, under the charismatic leadership of one visionary ideologue, harnessed feelings of resentment and rage. And, like the Nazis, the Brotherhood provided a range of paths to involvement for potential supporters. Both promised their adherents the chance to belong to revivalist institutions and the prospect of material betterment. The Brotherhood was especially successful in setting up a network of social and economic support groups that simultaneously nurtured a feeling of embattled solidarity and provided a route to greater radicalism. Indeed, al-Banna made the linkage explicit himself, organizing his followers in 'falanges' modelled on Franco's and expressing admiration for Hitler's Brownshirts. The embrace of violence central to fascist groups also became integral to the Brotherhood's organization, with the establishment of a 'secret apparatus' (*al-jihaz al-sirri*), which engineered a series of assassinations.

Al-Banna was himself killed in 1949, probably on the orders of the Egyptian government, but the work he had begun was continued and intensified by the man who, perhaps more than any other, has been Islamism's principal ideologue.

Sayyid Qutb (1906–66) was born, like al-Banna, in Egypt, and in the same year. Like al-Banna he received a traditionalist religious upbringing and exhibited precocious intelligence. He also went on to university in Cairo and then to a position with the Egyptian Ministry of Education. But while al-Banna's hostility towards the West was hardened by what he witnessed in Egypt, Qutb's was all the more intense because of the year he spent in America.

Qutb's time in the US was hardly, to contemporary eyes, a journey into decadence. He spent most of his time studying at the Colorado State Teachers' College in Greeley, a town which, given that it banned the sale and consumption of alcohol, might have been expected to recommend itself to the pious young Muslim visitor. But Qutb was horrified by what he saw as the emptiness of American life, the narrow materialism, the shallow hedonism, the cultural impoverishment and the headlong pursuit of commercial advantage rather than the cultivation of purer and more austere virtues. The American, and for that matter originally English, practice of enjoying private lawns and gardens outside houses was considered by Qutb to be striking evidence of a culture of greed. And watching young Americans dancing, at a church social, to the strains of 'Baby It's Cold Outside' inspired him to a furious philippic against the bestial carnality of Yankee youth. In his book, *The America I Have Seen*, he denounced the spectacle:

> They danced to the tunes of the Gramophone, and the dance-floor was replete with tapping feet, enticing legs, arms wrapped around waists, lips pressed to lips, and chests pressed to chests, the atmosphere was full of desire.

American women were animalistic temptresses:

> The American girl is well-acquainted with her body's seductive capacity. She knows it lies in the face, and in expressive eyes and thirsty lips. She knows seductiveness lies in the round breasts, the full buttocks, and in the shapely thighs and sleek legs. She knows all this and she does not hide it.

A half-fascinated, half-horrified reaction to Western women is a common Islamist trait. A fear of female sexuality, and independence, forms an integral part of Islamist thought: from the 9/11 hijackers who spent their last nights at strip clubs but gave precise instructions on how their bodies must not be sullied by female contact, to the insistent demand that their own women veil themselves completely from men's sight. Qutb's reaction to America, however, went far beyond just horror at a lack of feminine modesty. He believed that Western culture was both intrinsically rotten and yet also a uniquely dangerous force – Islam's greatest enemy – which had to be defeated if the purification of the Muslim world were to succeed. In his own revolutionary manifesto, *Milestones* (1964), he argued that: 'Western civilization is unable to present any healthy values for the guidance of mankind. It knows that it does not possess anything which will satisfy its own conscience and justify its existence ...'

Qutb's answer to the spiritual emptiness of the West, and indeed his challenge to his Muslim brothers, was a call to embrace a new world order based on submission to a sublimely rigid conception of Islam:

> If we look at the sources and foundations of modern ways of living, it becomes clear that the whole world is steeped in Jahiliyya [pagan ignorance of divine guidance], and all the marvellous material comforts and high-level inventions do not diminish this Ignorance. This Jahiliyya is based on rebellion against God's sovereignty on earth: It transfers to Man one of the greatest attributes of God, namely sovereignty, and makes some men lords over others. The result of this rebellion against the authority of God is the oppression of His creatures ...
>
> The Islamic civilization can take various forms in its material and organizational structure, but the principles and values on which it is based are eternal and unchangeable. These are: the worship of God alone, the foundation of human relationships on the belief in the Unity of God, the supremacy of the humanity of man over material things, the development of human values and the control of animalistic desires, respect for the family, the assumption of the vice-regency of God on earth according to His guidance and instruction, and in all affairs of this vice-regency, the rule of God's law [sharia] and the way of life prescribed by Him ...
>
> In the scale of God, the true weight is the weight of faith; in God's market the only commodity in demand is the commodity of faith. The highest form of triumph is the victory of soul over matter, the victory of belief over pain, and the victory of faith over persecution.

Qutb believed that Islam was a true, complete and total answer to all life's problems and dilemmas. He was convinced that the world was as pressingly in need of salvation as it had been before the birth of Islam. *Jahiliyya*, or barbarity, was the phrase used to describe the ignorance of the pagan tribes in the

Arabian peninsula against whom Muhammad battled to establish his faith. Qutb believed that both the leaders of the
Western world and the nominally Muslim rulers of his own
time were sunk in similar ignorance and barbarity. It was
against this contemporary *jahiliyya* that Islamism was to do
battle. Qutb believed in the creation of a vanguard, or *Tali'ah*,
of Islamist warriors to carry the fight to the enemy. He himself argued that 'those who have usurped the power of God on
earth and made His worshippers their slaves will not be dis-
possessed by dint of Word alone'. And he made good on his
promise.

The political ferment of the postwar Middle East gave
Qutb and his confederates the chance to move from theory to
practice. When the Egyptian monarchy, itself a prime example
of an elite in the grip of *jahiliyya*, was overthrown in 1952 by
a group of army officers led by, among others, Gamal Abdel-
Nasser, the Islamists saw an opening.

Qutb's transition from theoretician to political agitator had
involved him joining the Muslim Brotherhood on his return
from America, and becoming editor of its official journal. The
Brotherhood believed that Nasser's revolution created the
potential for Islamist advance. But the Brotherhood and its
supporters were to be disappointed. Nasser's plans for Egypt
did not include the implementation of sharia law and the
embrace of other fundamentalist tenets. For Nasser, indeed for
many other Arab leaders of his temperament and generation
who were coming to power at that time, nationalism and
socialism were more powerful impulses than Islam.

The Brotherhood reacted to what it saw as Nasser's apostasy
by choosing itself to follow a path of revolutionary activism.
But while the Brotherhood was ready to embrace violence, it
was not strong enough to withstand the Egyptian state. After a
failed attempt on Nasser's life, the movement was proscribed.
Qutb was imprisoned, while other Brothers scattered across the

Arab world. Nasser's acts were intended to crush Islamism as an ideological alternative to his regime. He intended to take Egypt, and with it the rest of the Arab world, on a path to greatness guided by socialist thinking and fuelled by nationalist feeling. Nasser's ideology of pan-Arabism was meant to be, like Islamism, an answer to his people's long years of decline.

Nasser's pan-Arab nationalism enjoyed its moment of triumph in 1956 when he nationalized the Western-owned Suez Canal and saw off a joint Anglo-French attempt to seize the prize back from his hands. But Nasser's promise of a revived and unified Arab nation at last triumphant over its enemies was shattered with the defeat of Arab armies at Israel's hands in the Six Day War of 1967.

Qutb did not live to see Nasser's defeat. He was hanged in an Egyptian jail in 1966. But the seeds of Islamist revolution had already been scattered, and sown, across the Muslim world. Activists from the Muslim Brotherhood were welcomed, and sheltered, in Saudi Arabia, where they taught, among others, Osama bin Laden. Bin Laden was subsequently to form his closest personal alliance with another disciple of Qutb's, the Egyptian doctor Ayman al-Zawahiri.

Muslim Brotherhood ideologues were active in every corner of the Arab world, from the Afghan hills through the Levant to the Maghreb. The Brotherhood was particularly energetic in Palestine, where its organization became known as Hamas. Like other totalitarian organizations, it has generated splits and factions, among the most famous being Hizb ut-Tehrir, a grouping formed in the 1950s by a Jordanian sharia court judge, Sheikh Taqi Uddin Al Nabahani.

Qutb's influence became felt across the Islamic world in the years following his death as Islamism grew in popularity and apparent relevance. In the Sixties and Seventies Arab rulers became wealthy on the back of burgeoning oil revenues but the societies over which they presided scarcely advanced. In the crudest test of international prestige, military competition, they found themselves continually bested by the tiny state of Israel. In intellectual terms, they generated no substantive body of new learning and certainly no technical innovation. In social terms they failed to deliver the opportunities that other rapidly developing nations could extend to their people. In economic terms, the oil failed to fuel wealth creation, with the entire Arab world's non-petroleum exports lagging behind those of Spain.

The critique mounted by Qutb, the judgement that apostasy, corruption and a surrender to Western values were holding the Muslim world back, had a seductive power. It played on feelings of loss, resentment, envy and wounded cultural pride. The spectacle of local elites maintaining a public piety while enjoying a life of private dissolution only encouraged feelings of anger and disaffection. Qutb's gospel had a particular power because it appealed to many sensitive, and intelligent, young Muslims. It has always been a mistake to believe that totalitarianism and terrorism find their primary followers among the crude, desperate, hopeless and impoverished. The cultivated undergraduates of 1930s Germany were seduced by Naziism just as many of the finest minds of the 1968 generation across the West were bewitched by Marxism.

It is instructive that the ring-leader of the 9/11 attack, Mohammad Atta, was an intellectual whose initial antipathy to the West was as much aesthetic as ideological. A graduate (in architecture) from an Egyptian university, he went on to study town-planning as a postgraduate in Hamburg. Atta's thesis dwelt on the transformation of the historic Syrian city of Aleppo. Atta saw in the growth of modern developments and the erosion of the distinctive and cherishable Arab cityscape a powerful metaphor for the dissolution of Islamic civilization under Western influence. For many young Muslims angered and disoriented by what they perceived to be cultural disintegration, the Islamism of Qutb and his followers provided both an explanation for decline and a programme for purification and renewal.

Qutb's influence, broadly acknowledged by modern Islamist fighters, is visible in the presence of Ayman al-Zawahiri by Osama bin Laden's side, and audible in the taped calls to restore lost Muslim glory issued by bin Laden himself. But Qutb is not the only Islamist ideologue to exercise a hold over contemporary minds.

Alongside al-Banna and Qutb, the third significant name in the growth of Islamism is Abul Ala Mawdudi (1903–79). Mawdudi was a journalist in British India who founded a sister organization to the Muslim Brotherhood in what was to become Pakistan. His group, Jamaat-i-Islami, was dedicated to the fundamental Islamist proposition that Islam was not so much a religion for private devotion as the source of a complete political system capable of competing with rival totalitarianisms for the minds of men. Mawdudi met, and collaborated with, Qutb, and both shared a view of contemporary Muslim society as decadent, worm-eaten by Western infiltration and ripe for remaking in fundamentalist form. Mawdudi developed an ideological vision of the ideal Islamist state. It was an explicitly totalitarian blueprint. As he explained it:

> a state of this sort cannot evidently restrict the scope of its activities. Its approach is universal and all-embracing. Its sphere of activity is coextensive with the whole of human life. It seeks to mould every aspect of life and activity in consonance with its moral norms and programmes of social reform. In such a state, no one can regard any field of his affairs as personal and private. Considered from this perspective the Islamic State bears a kind of resemblance to the Fascist and Communist states.

Mawdudi sought to elevate his vision above its totalitarian rivals by also stressing its differences – the equality that all would enjoy within its precincts, the beauty and balance achieved by a divine ordering of affairs – but the concrete reality of his vision only reinforces its fundamentally repressive nature. Non-Muslims would be second-class citizens, sharia law strictly enforced, and society would be established on a basis that was 'the very antithesis of Western secular democracy'.

Mawdudi's thought does admit accommodations with modernity. He allowed a place for a quasi-democratic consultation process (*shura*) in the governance of his ideal state. And he maintained that his vision was radically progressive in the equality it offered all believers, with no Muslim set in arbitrary authority over any other. But both these positions have to be viewed in the context of Mawdudi's belief that ultimate sovereignty rested with God alone. It was by his unalterable rules and in accordance with his perfect revelation that society was to be ordered. Down to the last detail.

Mawdudi died in 1979. Ironically, for a thinker who had devoted his life to purging the Islamic world of the toxic influence of Westernization, his last days were spent in Buffalo, New York, undergoing treatment for kidney disease. His movement, Jamaat-i-Islami, has campaigned for the establishment of a fully Islamic state in Pakistan, oscillating between occasional involvement in the constitutional political process and revolutionary activity. But Mawdudi's influence has not been restricted to Pakistani politics. His arguments for political Islam, and his call for Muslims to struggle towards the establishment of truly Islamic governance everywhere, continue to resonate. Indeed they have a more powerful hold today over Muslim intellectuals and leaders than perhaps ever before.

Al-Banna, Qutb and Mawdudi were all followers of what we understand by Sunni Islam, but support for Islamism is not restricted to Sunnis. There is also a powerful tradition among some Shia Muslims in favour of totalitarian Political Islam.

In Shi'ite Iran, the Muslim Brotherhood found a kindred

spirit in Navvab Safavi (1924–55), founder of the Devotees of Islam. Safavi was, like al-Banna and Qutb, a determined opponent both of Westernization and of what he saw as apostate Muslim rule. He encouraged his followers to bring about a wider political awakening, and the advance of Islamist rule, through the use of violence. His supporters also directed assassination attempts at those they considered responsible for importing alien secular influences.

The current conflict in Iraq has pitted Sunni Islamists against the majority Shia population, but there is a long-standing tradition of Shia–Sunni cooperation among Islamists. Iran has harboured some of Al Qaeda's own Sunni fighters and has been a consistent backer of Sunni Islamists among the Palestinians. These links go back to Safavi's time. He visited Egypt and Jordan in the 1950s to cement closer links with the Muslim Brotherhood and was a strong advocate of direct support for violent resistance against Israel.

Safavi was himself, like Qutb, eventually executed by the secular authorities. But his message did not die with him. One of the Islamists who protested against Safavi's death in 1955 was a cleric called Ruhollah Khomeini. Khomeini was to have his own run-ins with the Tehran authorities and was imprisoned before being driven from the country. But Khomeini was to take exquisite revenge on those who had executed his mentor and tried to extinguish his message. Twenty-four years after Safavi was killed, the rage that Khomeini had been compelled to nurse in exile eventually provided Islamism with its long-awaited revolutionary moment.

The Dawn is Crimson Red

The Iranian revolution of 1979, like the French Revolution of 1789, was a moment that grew into a model. Islamist dreams of power before 1979 had been desert mirages; after 1979 Islamism had a mountain fortress.

Iran's experience stands as a template for Islamist advance. The events that led up to the revolution show us just how Islamism can acquire a hold on political power. The variety of Western responses to the revolution show us how Islamism can draw strength, and admirers, when it exposes the weakness of its enemies. And the resilience of Islamist rule in Tehran demonstrates how difficult it has been for the West to develop an appropriate response to the jihadi challenge.

Before 1979 Iran was a Western client state. Like Saudi Arabia and Egypt today, it was an autocracy run by one family with a network of cronies sharing in the spoils. Iran's oil wealth in 1979, like that of the Gulf states today, meant that

the West took an indulgent view of the ruling family's governing style.

But there were other reasons, beyond commercial calculation, that inclined the West to favour Iran before 1979. In the
global struggle between the free world and communism the
West felt it could not afford to be too fastidious about who its
allies were. If an autocratic ruler wished to enlist on the
Western side in the Cold War, tough questions about human
rights records were seldom asked. The logic was simple. If the
country in question actually fell to communism then slaughter
and repression were certainties (look at Vietnam and
Cambodia). Better to keep a nation in the Western camp, to
check communism's global advance. And, if brutality was
perpetrated by one of your clients it would probably be only a
temporary expedient designed to maintain a ruler's position.
Better that than the systematic implementation of brutality, as
part of an ideological programme for remaking society, which
communism would inevitably entail.

This whole approach to supporting unsavoury regimes as a
bulwark against the greater evil of communism was memo-
rably and pithily summarized by one American statesman with
the line, 'He may be a sonofabitch, but at least he's *our*
sonofabitch.'

The Shah of Iran was the West's sonofabitch in the Cold
War, just as the Saud family and the Mubaraks of Egypt were.
And the latter continue to play that role today, except that they
are now propped up as bulwarks against Islamism rather than
communism. The irony of that position will be explored in
greater depth later. But it will not be lost on the reader how
unattractive the West must inevitably seem to uncommitted
eyes when it leaves its interests to be defended by corrupt
autocrats.

The Shah's regime may have been underwritten by Western
support, but its day-to-day authority rested on an apparatus of

repression. The Savak secret police kept order and were admired by rival autocracies for their exemplary ruthlessness and efficiency. But all their ruthlessness, all the Shah's wealth, and all the West's influence could not prevail against a single cleric with a tape recorder.

Ayatollah Ruhollah Khomeini, driven into exile by the Shah's forces for his Islamist activities, found a refuge of sorts in Seventies Paris. And from his French retreat he issued a series of calls to prayer, and arms, to the subject people of Iran. His words were recorded in the West, and transmitted across Persia, to a population ready to believe that the time for cleansing had come.

Iran in 1979 was a land where oil wealth flowed almost exclusively into the accounts of the powerful, where free political activity and democratic opposition were effectively suppressed, and where the promise of Western freedom was denied by the reality of Western complicity in oppression. The Iranian people were hungry for change. And the Islamists, led by Khomeini, were ready to feed that appetite. But it is important to note that the movement to unseat the Shah was not a self-consciously Islamist revolution from top to bottom. Far from it.

The Islamists played a role in 1979 similar to that which the Bolsheviks played in 1917. They were simply the most ruthless of all the forces that worked together to bring about revolution, and as the most ruthless of all the forces, the revolution soon became theirs alone.

Among those agitating to remove the Shah in Seventies Iran were communists, socialists, liberal democrats, non-Persian minorities and even disaffected technocrats. The revolution itself was, initially, viewed as much as a communist or socialist-inspired phenomenon as a religious event. But while the Islamists were capable of making an accommodation with the political Left, and indeed co-opted some of its slogans and grievances, they only really supported the socialists as the rope supports the hanged man.

Once the Shah's regime had been deposed the Islamists moved fast to consolidate their hold on power in Iran, a grip that has remained remarkably solid for a generation now. Islamism rapidly established its ruling characteristics. Iran faced the imposition of religious law, the consolidation of effective power in the hands of a clerical elite, the restriction of civil liberty in line with a totalitarian vision of Islam. It also became one of the world's most aggressive state sponsors of terrorism.

The new Iranian regime quickly signalled its unwillingness to play by the West's rules by, among other steps, taking hostage the staff of the US Embassy in Tehran. This was not just a tweaking of the Great Satan's tail, it was an intoxicating rewriting of the principle of sovereignty in line with Islamism's extravagant claims. The earth belonged to Allah. At last His disciples were advancing His rule over a blessed portion of it. The idea that even a few square yards of recently liberated Islamic soil should still hold out against submission to Allah was intrinsically offensive. And so it must be occupied to show that there were no limits to Islam's advance.

The West's initial responses to the Iranian revolution only reinforced the sense of exhilaration among Islamists. When the Americans, under President Carter, first tried to launch a mission to rescue their citizens it ended in military humiliation. The spectacle of the West humbled and a deliciously anti-rationalist force in the ascendant was all too much for some Western intellectuals. The Iranian revolution was welcomed by thinkers on the left such as Michel Foucault as an exalted moment. His response to radical Islam's advance was ahead of its time, but was to become, in its own way, prophetic.

As the Islamists entrenched their hold over Iran they also provoked, and sought to provoke, reactions from all their rivals. The bloodiest reaction to their takeover of power was the war that followed between Islamist Iran and its Ba'athist neighbour, Iraq.

The Iran–Iraq war was a conflict that elicited from Henry Kissinger the most bleakly witty of all his foreign policy observations. 'A pity,' he opined, 'they can't both lose.' But despite the appearance of studied, cynical detachment implied by those words the actual approach of the West to the conflict was compromised, dangerous and ultimately self-defeating. America, Britain, and indeed most Western powers ended up either actively or passively supporting Iraq in this conflict.

The rationale was understandable. Saddam might have been a psychopath but he was our psychopath. His regime was at least prepared, apparently, to play by rational rules. It did not seek to foment transnational revolution, nor was it leading a millenarian revolt against the West in the name of eternal truths. Instead it was happy to buy and sell, trade and badger in the manner of so many other autocracies with which the West had done distasteful business. One might have thought that after seeing where backing the Shah had led them, the West would have second thoughts about weighing in behind Saddam. But instead the West was happy to reinforce its own failed policy, supporting a second blood-stained autocrat as a bulwark against totalitarianism, precisely because the first one had so signally failed.

The decision to leave the fight against fundamentalism to a morally compromised autocracy was a grave strategic mistake and one that the West has gone on making. But it was not the only error of which the West was guilty in its response to the Iranian revolution. There were two other significant episodes that sent fatal signals of weakness, and set a pattern for the future.

In 1983–4 American troops were deployed to Lebanon as part of the complex process of seeking to stabilize that nation

One of the most significant forces in Lebanese politics was, and remains, the terrorist organization Hizbollah (Party of God), which is funded, and directed, by Iran. A suicide bombing carried out by Hizbollah terrorists in October 1983 succeeded in killing 241 American troops, part of the US forces then operating in Lebanon, as well as 58 French troops. At that time suicide bombing was a novel, and disturbing, terrorist tactic. And also at that time, the shadow of Vietnam still hung over American political calculations, so there was an inbuilt reluctance to allow foreign military commitments to become too entrenched, or to expose American troops to grave risks at the hands of desperate insurgencies. And so America withdrew its forces.

In the late 1980s a British writer, Salman Rushdie, published a powerfully charged novel, *The Satanic Verses*. Rushdie was acknowledged as one of the most inventive English prose stylists. His novel *Midnight's Children* had won the Booker Prize and he was known for his creative interweaving of historical fact and fantastic invention, the reworking of myth and its application to contemporary life. *The Satanic Verses* involved some creative reworking of Islam's founding narratives, just as *Midnight's Children* had relied on a poetic rereading of the fate of India's own foundation myths. But it was Rushdie's tragedy that the jury that delivered the most resonant verdict on *The Satanic Verses* was not one composed of Booker judges but rather a body of Islamic jurists.

Fundamentalist Islam was gravely offended by the depiction of the Prophet and his revelation in *The Satanic Verses*. It was particularly offended that this work should have been penned by a man brought up in the faith. For an infidel to profane the Word in this way would have been bad enough, but for a Muslim to turn not just apostate, but enemy, in this way was truly terrible. It was a crime that required exemplary punishment. For if apostasy, and worse, mockery of the faith, was not

punished, and seen to be punished, then what was to stop th
faithful questioning and subverting the faith that demande
total submission from them?

And so fundamentalist Islam's mountain fortress, Iran
delivered judgement on Rushdie. And that judgement, o
fatwa, issued on 14 February 1989, demanded no less tha
Rushdie's death. And lest anyone be inclined to think that thi
call was a purely symbolic utterance, calculated to play to th
gallery but meant to be ignored by sophisticates in the West
the Iranian authorities offered a cash reward for anyone wh
actually succeeded in carrying out the sentence of death.

It might be thought that a religious leadership certain of it
faith and confident in its virtue would have expected the sen
tence to be carried out by an individual who was motivated b
religious zeal alone. Surely, if the jurists were right in thei
interpretation of the faith, such a murder would be so pleasan
in the eyes of their God that the killer's salvation would b
secured by the very act of enforcing the fatwa. But, whateve
the theological calculations, it was clearly thought necessary t
add a financial incentive as well. Just as, to this day, the suicid
bombers of Palestine are offered a financial inducement to sac
rifice themselves, usually by men careful never to risk them
selves or their own children in a cause that they nevertheles
maintain guarantees eternal bliss and sure salvation.

In any case, the seriousness with which sentence was passe
on Salman Rushdie was never in doubt in the mind of the the
Conservative British government. Rushdie was given round
the-clock police protection and had to spend the next ten year
sleeping in a variety of safe houses to preserve his own life.

What was most striking about the nature of the threat tha
Rushdie faced was the extent to which his fellow countryme
made themselves accomplices in the campaign against him
Rushdie's book was burned in public ceremonies by those wh
professed sympathies with fundamentalist Islam. An attemp

was made to argue that the precepts of Islamic law should be respected, and implemented, in Britain and an organization, the Muslim Parliament, part-financed by Iran, was set up to advance the case that Koranic authority should prevail in matters affecting Muslims. Several cultured, and cultivated, British citizens stepped forward to excuse or justify the fatwa against Rushdie and support the totalitarians in Tehran against their countryman who was under attack for exercising the creative freedom cherished by all artists. One of the most prominent was Iqbal Sacranie, knighted in the Queen's Birthday Honours in 2005, who proclaimed that death was 'perhaps too easy' for Rushdie.[2]

The British state's response to this feline semi-endorsement of murder from Mr Sacranie has been revealing. The organization he subsequently set up, the Muslim Council of Britain, has been accorded a privileged position as the most trusted voice of Muslim opinion within the United Kingdom. But Mr Sacranie, and his organization, have never had their legitimacy validated by any democratic test. The position currently enjoyed by Mr Sacranie, who was knighted in the same Honours List as the Chief Rabbi, deserves closer scrutiny. But it is enough to note at this point that the reaction of the British state to Mr Sacranie's judgement on Salman Rushdie was to validate Mr Sacranie's position and accept his agenda.

While some Islamists tested the resilience of Western culture with their rhetorical attacks on Mr Rushdie himself, others concentrated their fire on the text. Many of those fundamentalists who claimed to be most offended by *The Satanic Verses* demanded that the initial offence caused by publication should not be compounded by issuing the work in paperback. This call, designed to test the willingness of leaders of 'progressive' opinion in the West to stand up for their professed principles, itself provoked interesting reactions. The Deputy Leader of the Labour Party, Roy

Hattersley, argued that no paperback publication should take place.[3]

There was a vital principle at stake here. Did the right to free speech deserve to triumph over the demands of religious zealots working hand-in-glove with a foreign totalitarian government? As far as one leading Labour politician was concerned in the late Eighties, free speech could go hang.

Less than twenty years later, in another row that pitted the defenders of free speech against the advocates of Islamic totalitarianism, another Labour politician was to respond in just the same way. Early in 2006, when Islamists reacted to the publication of some Danish cartoons that they believed impugned their faith by organizing riots and burning down embassies, the British Foreign Secretary apologized for the cartoons.[4] Like Roy Hattersley a generation before, Jack Straw gave Islamists exactly what they had been asking for – a validation of their belief that the West lacked both the strength and the will to defend its core values when they came under sustained attack. The lessons that are to be drawn from the publication of the Danish cartoons are important, and deserve closer study later in this book. But they have to be mentioned here because the Rushdie affair first demonstrated what those who protested against the cartoons already knew – the weakness of the West when it comes to defending its foundational principles.

In that sense the Rushdie episode was powerfully symbolic: it emphasized the rottenness of Western elites. If the West's leaders could not be relied on to defend civilization from a cultural attack launched by Islamists, then there was every reason for Islamists to believe that the future lay with them. And the Rushdie episode was just one of the three crucial responses to Iran's advance in the Eighties that confirmed in Islamist eyes the inevitability of their victory.

The West might enjoy massive military dominance, it certainly possessed huge economic power, and its cultural reach, through film, music, global brands and the international media, might seem total. But all this strength was built on the weakest of foundations.

What did military might matter without the will to prevail and the stamina to sustain a conflict over time against an implacable foe? And didn't the American retreat from Lebanon, in the face of suicide bombing, prove that the fighter armed with Islamist fervour was capable of defeating even the strongest Western force?

What did Western economic power count for if it depended so heavily on the flow of Middle Eastern oil and therefore rested on support for unsavoury regimes such as Saudi Arabia and, as it turned out, Iraq? How could the West ever hope to capture the minds of the Arab peoples, and others further afield, with the promise of democracy when it relied on hated tyrants to do its dirty work? Faced with such hypocrisy, the way was clear for Islamist victory in the battle of ideas and the struggle for hearts and minds.

And what did Western cultural reach matter when Western cultural confidence was so brittle? When put to the test by the Rushdie affair, Western leaders responded by either accepting Islamist demands or co-opting into their counsels those who pressed an agenda ultimately sympathetic to Islamists.

The lesson of the first decade of Islamist rule in Tehran was clear to Islamists everywhere – the future was there to be won. And in the next decade that was what Islamists everywhere sought to do.

4

The Weightless Decade

W. H. Auden described the 1930s as a 'low dishonest decade'. Would that he had lived to see the 1990s. This was the decade in which the West forgot itself.

The 1990s began with a hymn to freedom. On Christmas Day 1989, Leonard Bernstein gave a concert in Berlin celebrating the fall of the Berlin Wall, culminating with the last movement of Beethoven's 9th Symphony, the Ode to Joy, with the chorus's word 'Joy' (*Freude*) changed to 'Freedom' (*Freiheit*). It was a fitting anthem for the collapse of communism and the reunification of Europe.

But the lessons of the struggle that had secured that new freedom and unity were soon forgotten. In the euphoria of the moment, the assumption grew that the West could lower its guard after decades of vigilance against communism. European countries, whose protection had in any case long been guaranteed by America, proceeded to cut defence budgets that were already dangerously inadequate. Spending on intelligence and security services diminished in tandem.

The embrace of a weightless security policy was justified by the belief that history had reached a point where liberal democracy now stood invincible. Francis Fukuyama's thesis, *The End of History and the Last Man*, published in 1992, was wilfully misinterpreted to lend support to the view that democracies were unprecedentedly secure. Fukuyama certainly argued that democracies had comprehensively outpaced all their intellectual rivals as proven successes in delivering what citizens wanted. He had not predicted an end to conflict between democracies and those who refused to accept their virtues.

But instead of asking themselves why democracies had triumphed against communism in the Eighties, and what lessons that held for underpinning future security against other threats, Western societies pursued a course of self-indulgence. The enjoyment of peace dividends was fuelled by the conviction that a new paradigm was emerging in which painless economic growth was guaranteed. Speculation in internet stocks saw millionaires emerge overnight on the basis of concepts rather than profits, borne along on the belief that technology had redrawn the rules of global competition. The nations of the European Union busied themselves with plans for monetary union and institutional deckchair-shuffling. In America the political debate descended into an interminable discussion of the President's private life.

And while the West partied, the world burned. In Yugoslavia the collapse of communism did not provide its citizens with a peace dividend. Instead it allowed old divisions, suppressed under one totalitarianism, to emerge in new and more dangerous forms. War broke out in Bosnia, with Serbs, Croats and Bosnian Muslims plunging their corner of the European continent into vicious communal conflict.

The EU responded to this crisis by declaring, in the immortal words of Jacques Poos, Foreign Minister of Luxembourg, that 'the hour of Europe has come'. Unfortunately for the people of the former Yugoslavia, Europe's hour was spent on the telephone explaining why it couldn't act to prevent a genocide on its doorstep. Instead of intervening to prevent Serb aggression against the infant Bosnian state, European troops were restricted to impotent observation. Calls for air strikes to stop Serb military operations in their tracks were frustrated by French and British ministers. Demands that an arms embargo be lifted, so that the Bosnian government could acquire the means to defend its people from the already extravagantly armed Serb forces, were rejected by the British Foreign Secretary on the basis that this would create a 'level killing field'.[5] We left the killing field conveniently tilted in favour of the aggressor, so that he could continue to enjoy untroubled dominance.

The moment at which all these policies came together – the restrictions on the capacity of Western troops to act, the refusal to stop Serb militarism, the insistence on depriving the Bosnians of the tools to defend themselves – was in July 1995 in Srebrenica. There Serb forces massacred five thousand Bosnian Muslim civilians while Dutch NATO troops stood by and watched.[6] A few weeks later the policy so long derided by British and French ministers, the lifting of the arms embargo and the use of air strikes against Serb forces, was implemented under US leadership. Within weeks the Serb forces were humbled and peace talks initiated. The cost of inaction had been horrendous, the loss of human life immense. The impression had been given that the West lacked the will, and the capacity, to act with resolution against aggression.

The perception of the West as weak in the face of determined opposition may have emboldened a variety of potential enemies, but the West's behaviour in Yugoslavia was studied particularly closely by Islamists. The unwillingness to commit to any lengthy military campaign, the uncertainty of so many when it came to defending essential values, and the reluctance to sacrifice present economic comforts for future security – all this reinforced the impression of cultural weakness exhibited by the West in its encounters with Iran during the Eighties.

But Yugoslavia was much more than another stage on which Western weaknesses were bloodily laid bare. The conflict in Yugoslavia, depicted so often in the West as a civil war between sides mired in 'ancient ethnic rivalries', was viewed in very different terms by modern Muslims.

They saw fellow Muslims betrayed by the West and left to the mercies of a self-consciously anti-Muslim force. Bosnia's elected leaders had been Muslims facing a Serb enemy that clothed its ethnic aggression in crusading rhetoric. As far as Muslims were concerned, the West did not begin to do enough to protect the Bosnians, who were asking only that the basic European right to self-determination be respected. But the West did not appear, to Muslim eyes, to consider it worth while to extend that basic universal right to Muslims who happened to live in Europe. And because the West had let them down, aid had come from elsewhere. Mujahideen volunteers from across the Muslim world rallied to the Bosnian side, and money came from Saudi Arabia.

Those most willing to support the suffering were among the most radical, and politicized, believers in a fundamentalist vision of Islam. For Islamists, Bosnia was a tremendous political opportunity. They could demonstrate to fellow Muslims that whereas the West could not be relied on, those who followed a fundamentalist path were always ready to defend their brothers in faith. For the Islamists, Bosnia provided another opportunity to give their followers direct combat experience, it won them allies and sympathizers in the heart of the European continent, it helped to establish forward bases for training and recruitment, and above all it reminded the Muslim world of the essential weakness of the West at a time of testing.

Many British Islamists have dated their radicalization back to the time of the Bosnian conflict. The simultaneous impact of a West unsure of itself and unwilling to defend its values, Muslim brothers betrayed and suffering, and Islamists ready to risk their lives in struggle, proved inspirational for those young British Muslims already open, for a variety of reasons, to the totalitarian temptation.

Important as the conflict in Bosnia was, however, it was not the only political development in the weightless decade that demonstrated Western weakness to Islamist eyes. The Nineties were supposed to be the decade in which the West established a 'New World Order', building over the ruins of communism with a new global architecture designed to safeguard human rights and entrench peace.

One of the first tests of the New World Order came from the West's own prodigal son, Saddam Hussein. Saddam's war against Iran had provided his regime with neither the oil wealth nor the military glory for which he thirsted. But he believed it had given him an insight into Western decadence. He judged, on the basis of the West's actions during that war, that Western nations lacked the stomach for direct confrontation and were unhealthily dependent on seeing the flow of Middle Eastern oil maintained. And so the temptation to launch his own modest military adventure became overwhelming. By annexing the tiny, family-run emirate of Kuwait, Saddam thought he could legitimately claim to be retrieving a lost Iraqi province, while also significantly boosting both his reserves and his prestige. He was emboldened along this route by what he thought were indications of benign indifference from American diplomats in the region. Whatever the reality of the signals sent at that point, the pattern of Western behaviour towards Iraq over the preceding decade would certainly have seemed encouraging towards Saddam.

Saddam, however, initially miscalculated the scale of Western response. In his anxiety to establish that the New World Order was more than a pious aspiration, George Bush assembled a formidable coalition to dislodge Saddam from Kuwait and restore the sovereignty of the plundered emirate. The ensuing assault on Saddam's forces in Kuwait provided the world with a vivid, and gory, demonstration of what American firepower could achieve. As an advertisement of American military muscle it was as graphic as any one could have imagined.

But, on a broader and deeper level, the First Gulf War was an even more potent advertisement of American political weakness. After the gunfire had ended, Saddam sat secure on his throne. To dare to take on the mightiest military machine in the world, and then not only to survive but to survive with his power base intact, was an undoubted victory in the eyes of many across the world. And what made Saddam's victory all the easier to proclaim was the way the West behaved after its first, all too easy, gains.

Why did the American-led coalition not press home its advantage after the initial exchanges by advancing on Baghdad and deposing Saddam, to remove any doubt as to who was the victor of this exchange?

One of the constraints on American action was the nature of the coalition it had assembled. In order to maximize support for the ejection of Saddam from Kuwait it had been necessary to publicly limit the war aims to just that, the removal of Iraqi forces. By placing the requirement to secure the widest possible international support for action above the need to maintain maximum freedom of manoeuvre in pursuit of its national interest and global security, America sent a worrying signal. It would allow the coalition to define the mission rather than ensuring that the mission defined the coalition. It placed the satisfaction of international *amour-propre* ahead of the proper application of *force majeure*.

Another of the constraints on American action was the shadow that Vietnam cast over so many of its leaders. An antipathy towards any protracted conflict was, understandably, deeply embedded in the approach of men like Colin Powell. Their preference was always for either a brief conflict or none at all. The limited war aim of simply ejecting Saddam from Kuwait was much more congenial than the more ambitious enterprise of pressing home an early advantage to then remove him from power altogether.

On the basis of these two important calculations about American power, Saddam and others drew two profound lessons. The first was that international alliances, protocols and laws apparently designed to sustain Western power actually limited the West's, and crucially America's, ability to defend global order. And the second was that America's military strength could be withstood, and indeed overcome, if one was prepared for a long-drawn-out conflict. Both these calculations were to become crucial in the years ahead.

It was not, however, enough for the West to advertise its political weakness by simply leaving Saddam in power. The West not only allowed a tactical victory to become a strategic defeat, it also precipitated a humanitarian tragedy. America and Britain, while declining to depose Saddam, nevertheless indicated to the Iraqi people that they should finish the job themselves. And so in the north and south, among the Kurds and Shia, insurrections were launched. The people of Iraq's Kurdish north and Shia south launched their rebellion in the expectation of Western support and help, both moral and material. But instead of a helping hand for Iraq's democrats, the West gave a free hand to Saddam's forces. Rallying his loyalist troops, and exploiting the helicopter resources he was permitted to retain by the coalition, Saddam proceeded bloodily

o suppress a rebellion which was, at its height, supported by a
majority of Iraq's people.

While Saddam launched another campaign in the long war
he was waging against his own people, the West stood by. The
West incited a revolt but then acquiesced in a massacre. Our
leaders invited slaves to lift the yoke from their necks, only to
et it be replaced by a noose.

It was not only in Iraq, however, that George Bush's
America and John Major's Britain were advertising to the
world the brittleness of the order in their New World. In
Somalia, American troops were dispatched to bring 'tribal
warlords' to heel and restore a measure of calm to a nation
judged strategically important. But tactical misjudgements and
a rising casualty rate compelled a rethink, and then a retreat.
The American slinking from Somalia did not just condemn
that nation to further years of lawlessness, it also cleared the
way for Islamist advance. The Islamists had in Somalia not
only a new theatre of operations but also another visible
demonstration of American irresolution, which they could,
and did, use to emphasize to their followers the terminal weakness of the enemy.

Britain's own terminal weakness, under John Major, was
being advertised in a different but no less telling way, much
nearer to home. For more than twenty years the British state
had been under assault from Irish republican terrorism. By the
late 1980s Margaret Thatcher's government had achieved a
military ascendancy over the terrorists. The use of lethal force
to interdict terrorist operations, as the SAS succeeded in doing
in Gibraltar and Loughgall, not only deprived the IRA of key
operatives, it sent a vital signal of resolution. Special Branch
operations had also succeeded in so thoroughly penetrating
and disrupting republican networks within Northern Ireland
that the IRA was effectively contained and was in the process
of being rolled back. Compelled to sue for peace, the IRA sent

a message to the British government, declaring: 'The war i over, we need your help on how to end it.'

But the British government that received that message wa materially different from the one that had inspired it. While i was Margaret Thatcher's ministry that had worn the IR/ down, it was John Major's that embarked on peace talks wit republicans. And the approach that Major's ministry too could not have been better calculated to display the weaknes of politicians in the weightless decade.

Major's government set a number of tests for Irish republi cans before public negotiations could begin, specifically relate to the decommissioning of weapons. Each of these tests wa subsequently set aside without any serious movement on th part of republicans. The traffic was all one way. The negotia tion process culminated, under Major's successor, in the eleva tion of terrorists to government office without any materia surrender of their military capability. Put to the test directl by a terrorist organization, the British state under Majo and then Blair, had shown itself incapable of setting, and the defending, a firm bottom line. The lesson was not lost o others.

The global reach of Western media has been mentione before in this book, evidence of one of the areas in whic Western civilization continues to overawe all potential com petitors. But the reach of the Western media, as we shall see increasingly serves the interests of the West's enemies. Britain' handling of its domestic terrorist problem in the Nineties wa watched with great interest by Islamists. It reinforced their view that while the West, as a whole, was decadent, there were par ticular weaknesses in Britain's political landscape that provide prospects for advance.

The attention with which Islamists monitored events i Northern Ireland was confirmed by one of Abu Musab al Zarqawi's lieutenants in an interview with *Time* magazin when he asserted that the Iraqi insurgency was encouraged in its efforts by the example of Northern Ireland. It didn't matter how much the West protested it was in the conflict for the long haul. Britain's response to Irish republicanism showed once again that Western nations didn't have the stomach for protracted campaigns, whatever the rhetoric uttered by Western leaders. If terrorists persist, terrorism will pay off.

In each of the examples so far cited in this chapter – Bosnia, Iraq, Somalia, Northern Ireland – the West has been shown to be either weak, temporizing or irresolute in the face of threats. The posture described throughout most of the 1990s was vividly apparent to the most determined enemy the West faced – Islamist terror. As Islamism's most prominent warrior has made clear himself. Speaking in 1998, Osama bin Laden said:

> We have seen in the last decade the decline of the American government and the weakness of the American soldier who is ready to wage Cold Wars and unprepared to fight long wars. This was proven in Beirut when the Marines fled after two explosions. It also proves they can run in less than twenty-four hours, and this was repeated in Somalia.

Donald Rumsfeld once argued that weakness was more provocative than strength. That has certainly been the case as far as Islamism is concerned – it has detected in our weakness a vulnerability that invites exploitation. But while the West's weakness has appeared all too provocative to Islamism, the nature of the emerging threat from Islamist terror was scarcely apparent in the late Nineties to most in the West.

In so far as jihad had any meaning, it was an antique phrase appropriate to Crusader history or John Buchan novels. The mujahideen were figures of more recent romance, contemporary versions of Kipling characters engaged in a modern great game against the Russians on the North-West Frontier.

And Middle Eastern terrorism? Well, that was all a consequence of the conflict between Israel and the Palestinians, a
conflict that was now well on the way to resolution thanks to
the Oslo peace process.

It seems incredible now to recall, but the greatest fear that
the West believed it faced on the eve of the new millennium
was a computer bug.

But the evidence of the growing threat from Islamist terror
was everywhere for those with eyes to see. Afghanistan was not
a picturesque adventure playground for men who would be
king, it was the secure training ground for recruits whose calling was mass murder. It had moved from subordination to one
totalitarianism, communism, through lawlessness to subjection
under another totalitarianism, the Islamism of the Taliban.
But its fate scarcely commanded attention.

And connections that were ominous indicators of trouble
to come were overlooked by all but a very few. The Islamist
takeover of the Sudanese government during the Nineties
scarcely troubled Western commentators. Only a very few
brave souls, such as the former Archbishop of Canterbury
George Carey, and the Conservative peeress Caroline Cox,
tried to alert the world to the consequences of tolerating an
Islamist government in Khartoum by campaigning to highlight
the jihad that government was conducting against its Christian
fellow citizens in the south of Sudan.

Very few made the connection between Khartoum's
Islamist government and the activities of Osama bin Laden, a
renegade Islamist from Saudi Arabia who found temporary
refuge in the Sudan and declared war on the US in 1998. When
American embassies were blown up in East Africa, and an
American ship was attacked off the horn of Africa, within
striking distance of Sudan, few public connections were made
with the self-declared warrior against America.

When the Clinton administration responded to these

provocations by bombing a chemical factory in Sudan the overwhelming public response was neither gratitude nor exasperation that the counter-attack was so trifling, but cynicism about the President's motives in launching any sort of military action while questions still swirled about the scandal in his private life. Instead of debating what should be done to counter a growing threat, the Western media regarded counter-terrorist activity as just another trick in the public relations playbook designed to divert attention from unwelcome domestic developments.

The real tragedy of such media cynicism was that the White House felt the need to abandon counter-terrorist activity lest it all be seen as a process inflamed to divert attention from other matters. Clinton was so terrified lest he be accused of endangering soldiers' lives to get him out of a tight corner that he pulled his punches militarily.

And so Osama bin Laden was reinforced in his view that America's response to his actions was conditioned, by the inherent nature of American democracy, to be fitful, irresolute and ultimately ineffectual.

The Western media in the Nineties may have prided itself on its savviness, aggression and lack of deference. Certainly all those characteristics were on display during the Lewinsky affair. But the vigour with which the Press pursued these very personal matters squeezed out concern with truly vital issues. More than that, the effect of cynical media scrutiny and commentary on the President's own actions made him less inclined to do what was right and necessary for fear of being misjudged by a media determined to view every act through the prism of personal scandal. The Lewinsky affair was an example of the weightless decade at its worst. Matters that were intimate, personal, ephemeral and marginal exercised a magnetic pull on the Western public attention and its analytical faculties.

Meanwhile, matters of real gravity, specifically the growth, advance and entrenchment of murderous totalitarianism, scarcely troubled commentators or editors – and precious few politicians.

There was one issue, however, at the end of the Nineties on which it was still relatively easy to engender both media and political agitation. There was one conflict that, while calmed for a period, still had the potential to inflame. And within that conflict there was one analysis, almost universally shared, that the media and political class believed held the answer to peace.

The tragedy was that that analysis, far from promising peace, only reinforced the momentum towards yet greater slaughter.

5

The Condition of Zion

In *The Times* on 11 September 2001 an article I had written the day before appeared on the op-ed page. In it I tried to analyse the logic behind the Israeli–Palestinian peace process. Israel, I argued, was being asked to give up land for peace. There was a name for this process, I suggested. Munich.

It was my contention in the article that a cruel deception was being practised on the Israeli people. They were being invited to surrender territorial security for pledges of future good conduct, real estate for promissory notes. But what made this already risky venture so very dangerous was that Israel's interlocutors were not individuals of proven good faith. They were parties that had, at various times, pledged themselves to Israel's total eradication. They were groups that used the resources and political space they had to inculcate Jew-hatred in their children and train their young men in terror. And, above all, they were organizations that believed that the ceding of Israeli-held territory was a step in an ongoing process, not part of an agreed solution. For the forces arrayed against Israel the withdrawal of Israeli defence forces from any territory was not to be seen as a magnanimous gesture to be matched with an equivalent gesture of good faith. It was a retreat, won by force of arms, secured by the persistence of terror, proof of the ultimate weakness of the enemy and an incentive to press yet harder against a buckling opponent. It was, like the surrender of the Sudetenland, a vindication of violence, a reward for those who issued threats, and a promise that future threats would yield yet greater rewards.

My view of the peace process was not widely shared. The principle that Israel must cede territory to, and treat with, leaders of terrorist organizations still in arms against its people was a fixed assumption of Western diplomacy and a given among Western commentators. The idea I put forward that morning, that Western pressure on Israel to drop its sword, and yield ground to terrorist leaders, might embolden and encourage further terrorism, was regarded as marginal and eccentric.

That afternoon, while Britons were at lunch and Americans on their way to work, Osama bin Laden unleashed his attack on New York and Washington. The single bloodiest terrorist assault of our time had taken place, after years of appeasement, denial and retreat. Yet very different conclusions were drawn by the dominant cultural voices in the West. The attack was interpreted, reinterpreted, excused and justified in the days that followed by a series of Western commentators who were happy to pass judgement on the assault before all its victims had even been identified, never mind buried.

America had it coming, not least given its support for Israel. A bully with a bloody nose, wrote one *Guardian* commentator, is still a bully. Surely now, the chorus rose, America under its new President will stop throwing its weight around where it's not wanted, and instead put real pressure on Israel to re-involve itself in the peace process, and make substantive concessions.

What this chorus of commentators either ignored or chose not to acknowledge was the timing of Osama bin Laden's plan for the assault on New York and Washington. His plan had been conceived while President Clinton was still in office, while America was still engaged in pushing the peace process, while Israel was still negotiating with the Palestinians. The assault had been planned, commissioned and launched before a single chad hung in the Florida air, while Democrats still occupied the White House and while the world was still insisting that Israel must give ground to terrorists. This attack was not an infuriated response to Western negligence of the Palestinian question. It was the calculated escalation of a conflict in which the West's pressure on Israel to treat with terrorists was simply another proof of weakness in the face of mortal threat – a weakness that invited yet further assaults.

Both before 9/11 and since, there has been persistent pressure on Israel to negotiate, to yield and to acquiesce in the million small surrenders of the peace process. That pressure springs from a specific conviction – the belief that Israel is central to the difficulties that beset the wider Middle East. And so it is. But not in the way the majority casually assume.

The conventional view of Israel's centrality to conflict in the Middle East puts Israel in the dock for frustrating the Palestinian people's legitimate desire for statehood. Israel is held to have illegally occupied Palestinian land, specifically the West Bank and Gaza, thus creating the single greatest obstacle to progress for the Palestinian people. This crime, it is argued, is the single greatest cause of anger across the entire Middle East, the Arab world and the wider Islamic community, enraging the citizenry and fuelling their drift to terror. If only Israel were to live up to its obligations to the Palestinian people, face down its own extremists, and clear the way for the creation of a Palestinian state, then the single greatest root cause of terror in the Middle East would be removed.

As we have already seen, it is ludicrously reductionist and misplaced to attribute Islamist terrorism, given its global reach and totalitarian nature, to one territorial dispute. But the prevailing analysis of Israeli responsibility for exacerbating regional tensions is also profoundly misguided.

It is important, first of all, to put Israel's position in historic context. Israel's neighbours sought to strangle it at birth. It has fought at least three conventional wars in which its enemies' prime aim has been the annihilation of the Israeli state itself. These assaults in 1948, 1967 and 1973 were repulsed only thanks to the bravery and tenacity of the Israeli people, who fought alone in their own defence.

After one of these wars – in 1967 – the Israeli government sought to provide the Israeli state with more defensible frontiers, occupying land that belonged to its attackers, Syria, Jordan and Egypt, in order to cement its own borders. In the preceding hundred years any number of states had acquired, and kept, land following wars of territorial aggression, from the initial German acquisition of Alsace-Lorraine in 1871 to the expansion of Greece and Serbia at Turkey's expense in the Balkan wars of 1912–13. In the aftermath of the Second World War, as borders everywhere were redrawn, the Soviet Union consolidated its own expansion at the expense of Poland by occupying for itself much of the land it first grabbed when it signed a non-aggression pact with Nazi Germany. In each of these historic cases countries profited from their own decision to launch campaigns of conquest.

In Israel's case after 1967 it was occupying land that it had secured only after other nations had tried to launch a campaign of conquest *against it*. They had gambled that they would destroy the Jewish people's only homeland, and they had lost. But what each had lost was only a sliver of its own territory.

It is important to recall, and now almost always forgotten, that the land Israel occupied was not, in any formal, legal, internationally recognized sense, Palestinian. It was Syrian, Jordanian and Egyptian territory. And what was striking about the people who lived on that territory, who were thought of as Palestinian, is the way they were treated between 1948 and 1967 by all Israel's neighbours. They were herded into, and kept penned up inside, refugee camps. To be used as human battering rams against Israel when the time came.

While Arab countries busied themselves expelling Jews after 1948, and Israel made enormous efforts to absorb every Jewish arrival fully into Israeli life, those same Arab nations that were so anxious to make themselves *Judenfrei* did next to nothing to provide their Arab brothers with a stable footing. Quite the opposite. The Palestinian people were kept in refugee camps, and in a state of expectation that they would soon be able to take over Israel. The United Nations acquiesced in this confirmation of second-class status, and underwrote the view of many Arabs that Israel's position was tenuous and provisional by maintaining these camps for refugees, rather than helping with resettlement in new Arab homelands, on the apparent assumption that the camps' occupants would soon be staking a claim to the land currently, and temporarily, occupied by Israelis.

It is striking also that no pressure was placed on Jordan, Egypt or any other Arab nation to help construct the institutions of Palestinian statehood during the long years when they occupied what has come to be considered Palestinian national territory. It is only following the occupation of that land by Israel that it has become considered imperative to transform that territory into a new, and distinct, Palestinian state.

What this melancholy tale of Palestinian neglect at the hands of Arab states demonstrates is the hypocrisy at the heart of so much Arab propaganda against Israel, propaganda that much of the world is inclined to take at face value. The leaders of Arab states, none of them until very recently with even the slightest claim to be called democrats, have exploited the plight of the Palestinian people as a way of demonizing Israel, and creating a force to drive Israelis into the sea.

If it were true that solidarity with the Palestinians was the primary political force motivating feeling among both Arab elites and Arab peoples, then we would have seen investment pour into building up schools, hospitals and democratic structures in the Palestinian territories during those periods when they were either under the control of Israel's neighbours or of Yasser Arafat's PA leadership. Which, of course, never happened. Money certainly has flowed from other Arab, and indeed Islamic states, into the Palestinian territories over the years. That cash has not been sent to build a state, but to destroy one.

The reason why Israel is hated by the rulers of so many Arab states, by the leaders of so many terrorist organizations, and especially by the world's Islamists, is not because of any specific crime against the Palestinians. In the eyes of all these individuals, and organizations, Israel's greatest crime is simply to exist at all. Israel's existence as an openly plural, explicitly Western, conspicuously successful democracy in the heart of the Islamic world is just too much to bear. And not just for the autocrats and fanatics of the Islamic world. It is too much for many in the West to bear too. Israel's success is a standing rebuke to so many of the assumptions cherished by the region's other leaders and the West's own radicals, that it inspires a hatred that can, and does, lead to irrationality.

In a region that is supposed to have been held back by colonialism, hampered by prejudice and crippled by years of exploitation, the single most successful nation is the one least favoured by nature. Israel's economic output, rate of growth, levels of employment, educational achievements, infant mortality and standard of public health care comprehensively outstrip all of its neighbours.

There are, of course, two significant differences between Israel and all its neighbours in the region. And one of them is not the existence of Western economic support. Egypt, the Palestinian Authority and Saudi Arabia have all, in their own way, benefited generously from the West's financial support.

No, the two significant differences are these. Israel has no oil or gas. But it is the only state where governments change as a result of democratic elections, the Press is free, the courts fair, the officials uncorrupt, contracts open and enforceable, and political opposition integral to the culture.

For all those whose narrative of the last sixty years places the West in the dock, finds capitalism and imperialism guilty of the greatest global crimes of our time, and lays the woes of the developing world at the door of the developed, the condition of Israel is a living refutation of all they stand for. For the leaders of all Israel's neighbours, Israel's success is a daily reminder of how they have failed their peoples.

If any dispassionate observer were to look at the region from Tangier to Tehran, ignorant of where national borders lay but concerned only with the material condition of the peoples he encountered, he would inevitably be forced to ask why not only the greatest prosperity, but also the most visible culture of equality, was found in the territory currently administered by the Israeli government. He would be compelled to ask why the standard of living was so much more enviable than anywhere else in that whole crescent, save for the palaces of a few favoured families. And it is to stop that question being asked, as it should be, with increasing strength and vigour, that the leaders of Arab nations are so eager to see the campaign against Israel's existence continue.

It is a campaign that they prosecute on every level open to them. To prevent their people asking why they are not as free,

or wealthy, as Israel's, the leaders of Arab opinion work sedu-
lously to paint Israelis as the authors of every wickedness, the
villains behind every conspiracy. That is why the Arab world
has recently witnessed an upsurge in anti-Semitism as vicious
and sustained as anything seen in Thirties Germany.

The text that calls itself *The Protocols of the Elders of Zion*,
cooked up by Tsarist agents to foment anti-Semitism in pre-
World War One Russia, is a forgery that claims to reveal a per-
fidious Jewish conspiracy to secure domination of the world.
It outlived its original creators to become a widely quoted
authority on Jewish malevolence in pre-World War Two
Germany. One might have thought that, after the horrors of
the Holocaust, the ideas behind the text, and indeed any reference to it, would have been unthinkable, but instead
Egyptian state television recently built a whole series for
national prime-time viewing on the premise that the *Protocols*
were true. The Syrian Defence Minister, Mustafa Tlass, has
published them for a credulous public.[7] And Hamas, the
Palestinian offshoot of the Muslim Brotherhood, helpfully
includes them in its constitution.

In the state-controlled media of almost every Arab nation,
Jewish figures have been depicted as bloodsuckers, poisoners of
wells, spreaders of disease, corrupters of youth, killers of children, whether for ceremonial or just straightforward sadistic
purposes, and, in a curious inversion which almost defies logic,
Nazis. This equation of modern Jewish figures with Nazis
might be intended to suggest that contemporary Israeli crimes
stand comparison with the historic atrocities of Hitler's
Germany, except that there is remarkably little acceptance
among Arab and Islamic elites that Hitler's Germany was actually guilty of any atrocities. The Iranian President, Mahmoud
Ahmadinejad, explicitly denies that the Holocaust took place.[8]
The Syrian President has allies who like to deny that the
Holocaust took place.[9] And the Palestinian President, Abu

Mazen, secured his doctoral thesis for work that also dispar-
aged the Holocaust.[10] Which is perhaps why he was so relaxed
that one of the Fatah candidates in the last Palestinian elections, that's to say one of those the world called moderates, was
known to his fellow electors as 'Hitler'.

This wave of anti-Semitism, only a sample of which can be
noted here, reflects the need felt across the region to demonize
and scapegoat Israel for the suffering of Arab peoples. The
people encouraging, funding and arranging most of that
demonization are, of course, the principal agents of the Arab
people's suffering, specifically the Arab people's own leaders.

Israel is central therefore to the troubles faced by the
Middle East because it points up the desperate condition in
which Arab and Islamic elites have left their people. In that
sense, Israel's continued existence serves to emphasize one
important strand in the Islamist critique of Arab elites. How
can the peoples of Allah have been allowed to fall so far behind
those who were their second-class subjects for so much of history? What further proof of the failure, apostasy and corruption of contemporary rulers is needed? And what more pressing cause can there be for Islamists than the reclamation of
land once consecrated to Allah and now defiled by Jewry's
presence?

Central to the Islamist programme for advance is the principle that any, and all, land once occupied by Muslims has to
be reclaimed for Islam. Ultimately, of course, the entire globe
has to be claimed for Allah, since he alone holds sovereignty
over this world. But there is an urgent need, in the first
instance, to show the infidel that the land he has removed from
Muslim hands will be restored to Islamic rule. For that reason,
the fate of Kashmir, Chechnya and even Andalucia haunts
Islamist minds. All of these are territories at the edge of the
Islamic world that have been prised from Islam's grasp,
whether at the point of a sword or by the stroke of a pen, in a

way that reinforces a narrative of Muslim decline. But none of these territories has quite the hold on the Islamist imagination that Israel has, for Palestine is a land not on the borders, but in the very heart of the Muslim world.

Islamists operate to a timescale, and in a thought-world, quite different from that which guides the actions of Western leaders. For them Israel's existence is an affront that demands to be effaced, but it is not a unique and novel challenge to their mission. Islamists recall previous occasions when the Levant was occupied by states that were a threat to the dream of Muslim unity, a breach in the seamless robe of the *umma*, the community of Islam. They remember that in the twelfth and thirteenth centuries Christians established kingdoms on the eastern shore of the Mediterranean, but those Crusader states only endured for a generation or two before they fell to Muslim arms. In the historic sweep by which Islamists judge events, the existence of Israel, still less than sixty years old, ranks alongside the establishment of those Crusader kingdoms. The expectation that Israel will fall, as the Crusader states fell, animates Islamist hopes. And the course of recent events only reinforces the Islamist conviction that Israel's existence is built on sand.

In the last ten years or so, as Islamists see it, Israel has been in retreat while their cause has advanced. When Israel withdrew from southern Lebanon this military retrenchment was not viewed as the necessary preliminary to a stable reordering of the region in which Israel's rights were to be respected as the grievances of its neighbours were addressed. Islamists instead saw it as evidence of military and political exhaustion, a retreat forced on Israel by the activities of their terrorist brethren in Hizbollah and its confederates.

By the same token, Ariel Sharon's withdrawal from Gaza was not seen as a redrawing of Israel's commitments, paving the way to the establishment of a new Palestinian state living in deserved peace alongside a secure Jewish nation. Instead it was

viewed as a vindication of Hamas's terrorist campaign, a victory
for Islamist arms that compelled Israel to retreat in disgrace
and disarray. Indeed, the ability of Islamists to present Israel's
withdrawal as proof of Hamas's success was a direct contribu-
tory factor to the Hamas triumph in the elections that followed.
Evidence of weakness in the face of Islamist action only succeeded in further strengthening the position of the extremists.
Land was surrendered in the hope of peace, but given the
nature of that surrender, as I argued sadly four years before, it
would only embolden those who were peace's enemies.

It is sometimes tempting for Western leaders to try, in every
sense, to distance themselves from Israel. The difficulties Israel
faces in dealing with terror are held to be specific to that country's geography, history and politics. The connection between
Israel's position and the challenges faced by Western nations
are held to exist only in so far as Israel's refusal to bend feeds
a resentment among Muslims that leads to trouble for the West
at home and abroad. The West's best interests, according to
this analysis, lie in putting distance between itself and Israel,
putting pressure on Israel to change its policies, and acknowl-
edging the view promulgated by Arab elites that Israel's actions
are at the root of current discontents.

But, as we have seen, stepping up pressure on Israel to
change its policies in the current climate has only had the effect
of encouraging terrorists further. Assenting to the critique
mounted by Arab elites means becoming an accomplice in the
construction of an alibi for their failures. And, in any case, in
Islamist eyes the connection between the West and Israel is
not a temporary geopolitical matter, capable of being affected
by the actions of any national leader. It is a profound, ideological, even spiritual link. When Osama bin Laden talks of
the Zionist–Crusader alliance he is not referring, in his quaint
way, to a current diplomatic accommodation between Israel
and the West, to be thought of in the same light as NATO in

the twentieth century or even the Dreikaiserbund of the nine-teenth. He and his fellow Islamists see today's Zionists, like the medieval Crusaders, as simply another manifestation of Islam's eternal enemy: the intransigent infidel. For them the contemporary Zionist–Crusader alliance is the expression of an underlying reality – Israel, like the rest of the West, lives by values utterly inimical to the totalitarian Islamist vision.

As far as Islamists are concerned the entire West is con-ducting a daily assault on the essentials of their faith. By upholding democracy, extending equal rights to women, per-mitting sexual licence, allowing the lending of money with interest, making laws without reference to the Koran, and gen-erally maintaining a pluralist and open society, the peoples of the West offer a continuing provocation to the faithful. And because the vigour of Western society, its commerce, industry and media, dangles temptation in the face of good Muslims the world over, it must be countered, and defeated. In this per-spective, just as the Crusades threatened the integrity of the Muslim world in medieval times, with the twin threats of mili-tary force and Christian proselytization, so today the West is mounting an insidious assault with its brute commercial power and gospel of freedom. Israel stands out primarily because it is such a provocatively sited forward base for these forces. In that sense, the Zionist–Crusader alliance is not an arrangement that either party can terminate, it is a description of a deep under-lying reality. Israel is an integral part of the West, a vessel for its values, an example of its virtues, and it is hated not for what it does but for what it is. The same holds true for the rest of the West. Islamism does not seek an alteration in Western policy per se, save as a transitional step in wearing down Western res-olution. Rather it looks to the defeat of the West as an idea and an ideal. It is a remarkably ambitious goal. But what makes it seem achievable is how weak the West's defences now appear.

6

Relative Values

I have examined why it is that Israel occupies a special place in the Islamist demonology, but it is worth while considering for a moment the peculiar place it also holds in contemporary Western radical thought.

For several years now, anti-Israel feeling has been a distinguishing feature of discourse on the radical left. It was not always so. In the years immediately following Israel's establishment its cause was enthusiastically championed by many on the left. Keeping faith with the Jewish people was an important element in keeping the anti-fascist flame burning. Anti-Semitism was a distinguishing mark of the unacceptable Old Right, whether it found expression in drawing-room slights or in Foreign Office manoeuvres. The vigour of the Israeli Labour Party, the idealism of the kibbutz movement and the vividly reactionary nature of many of the Arab regimes ranged against Israel all reinforced the sense of solidarity most on the left felt for the infant Jewish state.

But that sympathy, strong as it was, began to ebb in the late 1960s. For many on the left, comfortable with Israel as a community of refugees and attuned to empathizing with the Jewish people as victims, the emergence of a proud and self-confident Jewish nation state capable of defending itself with élan on the battlefield was discomfiting. What deepened the discomfiture for many was Israel's occupation of territory that went beyond its 1948 boundaries. They detected in this defensive manoeuvre echoes of traditional power politics and the shadow of colonialism.

The change in attitudes towards Israel was driven, however, as much by changing intellectual currents in Europe and America as by altered frontiers in the Middle East. The emergence of a New Left alongside the student tumults of 1968 changed the way future generations expressed their idealism. A combination of influences reshaped the radical mind The traditional demands of social democracy, such as full employment, welfare rights and greater wage equality, were increasingly being satisfied by parliamentary means. The historic pull of Soviet communism on young imaginations had been undermined by Khrushchev's denunciation of Stalin in 1956, further damaged by the Russian invasion of Hungary, and all but destroyed by the crushing of the Prague Spring.

In the place of traditional social democracy and conventional communism a variety of new trends drove leftist thinking. The thinkers of the Frankfurt School revived Marxism as primarily a cultural rather than an economic movement. In place of anger at traditional capitalism, scorn was directed at the reigning value systems of the West. Bourgeois conformity and respect for authority were held up as repressive checks on the human spirit. The eternal rebel was elevated as the hero of the times.

In parallel with these trends, the twin processes of civil

rights agitation and the growth in national liberation movements across the developing world altered perceptions of
where struggle lay. Instead of history being viewed as a matter
of class conflict, it was increasingly seen as an anti-colonial,
anti-Western process. The place of the proletariat in the affections of the Left, as a group onto whom fantasies of revolution
could be projected, was assumed by the non-Western peoples
of the globe. In place of Rosa Luxemburg and Vladimir Lenin,
the icons of struggle became Ho Chi Minh and Che Guevara.

The working out of these trends was often beneficial. The
struggle against apartheid benefited from the infusion of radical energy that a new focus on the difficulties of the developing
world gave. But the consequences of these trends for the
Middle East were simultaneously more complex, and tragically malign. Israel moved from a place of safety, secure in the
affections of the Left, to a position in the dock, arraigned for
complicity in the crimes of the West. The Israel that liberated
its people from the grip of terrorists at Entebbe airport was a
swaggering colonial adventurer. The Israel that moved from
the agrarian self-sufficiency of kibbutz days to commercial
expansion and market success had surrendered the right to be
romanticized, sold its soul to the bourgeoisie. The Israel that
had moved beyond mourning its tragic past, and now made
heroes of those who defended its borders, was no longer a
nation of victims to be pitied, but of militarists to be shunned.

And set against Israel were rebels ripe for idealization. The
appetite for struggle that stirred young European hearts could
be satisfied by attaching oneself to the Palestinian cause. That
such attachment, at its most passionate, led the young
Germans of the Red Army Fraktion who claimed to be
angered by their nation's Nazi past to go on to murder Jews
was an irony too dark to be dwelt on.

During the 1970s the wider indulgence extended to
Palestinian terrorists set an unhappy precedent that gave an

early indication of the West's long-term weakness. From the fate of Leila Khaled, released by Edward Heath just one month after she was apprehended for her part in a terrorist hijacking,[11] to the German government's complicity in the release of the men responsible for the Munich massacre, the pattern of Western government behaviour in the early Seventies was almost precisely calculated to encourage those within the Arab and Islamic world who believed that violence was the most effective means of prosecuting their goals. And ominous as the attitude of Western governments was for the future, more worrying still was the intellectual momentum behind the anti-Western currents operating at that time. During the Seventies the celebration of anti-Western rebellion tended to be restricted to those circles that were self-consciously at one radical remove. It was a mark of distinction, and of distance from the mainstream, to celebrate guerrilla movements and join any of the fringe groupings, from the IMG to the SWP, that occupied determinedly revolutionary territory.

But qualities exclusively associated with the radical Left in the Seventies soon came to permeate the wider Left in the years that followed. The collapse of confidence in social democratic circles, and the dominance of centre–right governments across the West during the Eighties, led to a broader realignment on the left. Just as the Marxists of the Frankfurt School had done, the broader Left moved its arena of struggle increasingly away from economic arguments and towards cultural ones.

In Britain there may have been symbolic last stands in defence of jobs, services and union rights during the miners' strike and around the abolition of the GLC, but the radical energy of the time was focused less and less on workers' struggles, and instead engaged in wider battles. Solidarity with Nicaragua, opposition to Pinochet, the marshalling of a separatist consciousness through the struggle for black sections within the Labour Party, the reinterpretation of the miners' dispute through feminist eyes with the celebration of the sacrifices made by the women's movement – all of these causes were evidence of a new orientation on the left. Politics changed from an argument about economic organization to a series of assertions of identity.

And even as the Labour Party itself, like other centre–left and social democratic movements, changed to take account of new electoral realities, so it, and the broader Left, retained their radicalism through the embrace of this new cultural politics.

Indeed, as Labour and the broader Left moved away from the economic policies of the past that had tied them to working-class constituencies, so they also distanced themselves from that part of the broad left coalition that was inclined to be culturally conservative, naturally patriotic and resistant to faddism. Instead, the Left became more and more a movement of those public-sector professionals, alerted to cultural issues during their university years, who were on a perpetual quest for new victims onto whom they could project their need to feel righteous anger.

For an increasing number over the years, the cause that has proved the most useful in satisfying this emotional need has been the Palestinian movement.

Clearly, the Palestinian people deserve a brighter future. Their claim to statehood is just and urgent. Their suffering has been heart-rending, their right to peace and security is pressing. They have been denied justice for too long. And there have been many in Israeli life and politics who have worked, tragically and wickedly, to frustrate Palestinian aspirations.

But the principal obstacles to the achievement of Palestinian statehood have been the reluctance of Israel's neighbours to contemplate the existence of a viable Palestinian state next to a secure Israel; their determination to use the Palestinian people as a hostage army against Israel; the Palestinian leadership's addiction to terrorism; that leadership's refusal to use the freedom, resources and space it has enjoyed to invest in any of the institutions of statehood or lay the groundwork for freedom; and, latterly, the hijacking of aspirations towards statehood by Islamists whose goal is not a liberated democratic state but a strict totalitarian theocracy. None of those points is raised, other than to be ritually dismissed, by those radicals in the West who have made themselves partisans of the Palestinian cause. Because their adoption of the Palestinian cause is driven by other factors.

There are any number of suffering peoples, many stateless, others betrayed by their countrymen, whose torment cries out to heaven for justice. From the Karen people, who are the victims of a genocidal campaign of violence by the national socialist Burmese government, to the Tibetan people whose culture and freedoms have been eradicated by communist China, from the persecuted Shia of Saudi Arabia to the democrats, writers and thinkers who languish as political prisoners in Cuba. But their causes receive scarcely a hundredth of the space in leftist discourse that the Palestinian cause enjoys.

During the protests against the Gulf War thousands marched to prevent Saddam Hussein being deposed. There were many striking factors to these demonstrations worthy of note, from the nature of the organizers to the willingness of so many to march in defence of a mass murderer continuing in office. But one of the most striking things about the march was that, alongside the countless banners demanding a stop to the war, only one other slogan appeared. And it appeared on nearly every other banner. It was the demand to 'Free Palestine'.

It might be thought appropriate to use a gathering of those politically committed to one cause to canvass support for others. But what is striking is how one cause, and one alone, dominates and excludes all others.

What will also have struck any shopper who has strolled along Oxford Street in the last year will have been the organized boycott outside one store, Marks and Spencer, focused on one issue, protesting against Israeli actions. Under Palestinian flags, the protesters attempt to dissuade passers-by from buying Israeli produce. There is, of course, a melancholy precedent for organized street protests designed to encourage the boycott of Jewish goods. But what is striking about this boycott, apart from the capacity of intelligent people sixty years on from the Holocaust to think that boycotting items just because they are Jewish is a good idea, is that of all the nations that could be singled out for criticism, it is Israel in the dock, and out of all the causes that might merit this type of support, it is the Palestinian cause that inspires this action.

It is also striking that when British academics recently tried to organize a boycott of one country that was held to have breached basic human rights, and therefore to have placed itself outside the realm of civilized discussion, that country was not China, not Zimbabwe, Cuba, Syria. It was, of course, Israel.

There is a reason why the Palestinian cause absorbs so much more political energy than any other campaign for justice, why it dominates the placards, speeches and statements when radicals mobilize, and why it drives other left-wing activity to the margins. It's not about them. It's about us.

The reason the Palestinian cause is so central to modern left-wing activity, and central in the peculiar way I have described, is because it is the contemporary rallying point for the dominant radical impulse of our time – anti-Westernism. And attachment to the Palestinian cause is an emotionally satisfying and morally exalted way of attacking Israel – the country that is the West's front line, the state that embodies Western values in a region and at a time where they are under particularly vicious assault.

Consider for a moment not just how much emotional energy support for the Palestinian cause absorbs, relative to so many other causes of concern, but also where partisanship for Palestine, and therefore opposition to Israel, has driven people. It is not just a matter of a few students recreating anti-Jewish boycott campaigns outside Jewish-owned department stores. A curious warping of public debate has taken place in which objective judgement, proportion and truth itself have been set aside in order to satisfy the need to put Israel, and the wider West, constantly in the dock.

Take just one episode from recent history – the Israeli Defence Force action in Jenin, Operation Defensive Shield. Jenin was a known centre of terrorist activity on the West Bank during a period when Israeli citizens were at particular risk from suicide bombings. In the days immediately before Operation Defensive Shield was launched, a suicide bomber in Netanya had killed 28 people celebrating Passover and another bomber in Haifa had murdered 14 others. These attacks were simply the latest, and most horrific, in a series of assaults launched from Palestinian Authority territory with the support of the PA leadership which had killed 87 and wounded more than 570 in the preceding months.[12]

The Israeli Defence Force entered Jenin with the specific aim of rooting out the organizers of this terrorist campaign. Their aim was simple: to defend their fellow citizens by targeting the men behind an offensive military campaign. But this straightforward act of self-defence was portrayed to the world as an atrocity. For the BBC it was 'a massacre'. For one *Times* foreign correspondent it was worse than Chechnya. For the editor of the *Guardian*, in his leader page, it was a crime every bit as horrendous as 9/11.

Let's pause for a second to consider what each of those

descriptions is meant to convey. A massacre? Surely that word can be used to describe only the callous and indiscriminate slaughter of relatively large numbers of innocents, whether by trickery or cruel brute force, as in Rwanda or Srebrenica? Chechnya? Surely the purpose of that comparison is to remind people of Russian tactics in razing entire cities to the ground, heedless of the consequences for the population, leaving thousands dead in their wake? 9/11? Well, anyone comparing an event to 9/11 must be trying to conjure up a picture of unique horror, the deliberate and terrifying slaughter of innocents, again with no thought given to the number of casualties caused, and motivated by the worst sort of fanaticism. Why else mention it?

So, what actually happened in Jenin? According to the Palestinian politician Saeb Erekat, speaking as the Israeli forces withdrew, 'How many people were massacred? We say the number will not be less than five hundred.' That figure was widely reported, and used as evidence that a massacre had indeed taken place. But had it?

The truth was eventually established in August 2002 following an exhaustive investigation by Rights Watch and the United Nations. The final fatality figures were 75 deaths: 26 Palestinian terrorists, 23 Israeli Defence Force soldiers and 26 civilians. This was not, by any stretch of the word, a massacre. It had been a difficult police action. The Israeli Defence Force had to work its way through booby-trapped homes, negotiate situations where terrorists were using civilians as human shields, and counter an enemy prepared to endanger other Palestinians in order to evade capture. In the process the IDF had to be bound by an ethical code that requires it to minimize the risk to innocent life. In the process of observing that code, IDF soldiers exposed themselves to proportionately greater risk. Which is why 23 of them died. And their posthumous reward? To be smeared across the world media as war criminals.

Jenin is only one of the most egregious examples of Israel's actions being twisted by the media, and represented by the radical Left, in order to make the victim the villain.

There are many reasons why individuals might delight in traducing Israel's position, particularly in the context of the ongoing conflict with Palestinian terrorism. For some people the opportunity to indulge the oldest hatred – anti-Semitism – in the new guise of humanitarian concern will have been too tempting to resist. For some people identification with the Palestinian cause will have allowed them the delicious thrill of solidarity with those who have made a profession of violence. The opportunity is there to show one's contempt for bourgeois mores, conventional authority and the whole apparatus of Western repression by rubbing shoulders with those whose most glamorous accessory is their Kalashnikov. The same impulse that led Leonard Bernstein to host a benefit for the Black Panthers,[13] that took the Mitfords to Berchtesgaden and Jane Fonda to Hanoi, now propels many into the arms of Israel's enemies. For some people, taking a leading role in public criticism of Israel will have won them approval in the circles that count – the progressive print media, the public service broadcast media, academia, publishing, the higher civil service, centres of radical thought, public sector grant-awarding bodies and prestigious cultural prize-giving juries.

But, whatever the impulse, this campaign against Israel is ultimately an exercise in undermining those who are in the front line of the ongoing war against the West.

Beyond the Front Line

There are particular reasons, beyond its front-line status, and beyond those explored so far, that explain why Israel occupies a special place in radical demonology. And those reasons impact directly on the capacity of the West to defend itself against assault, not least from the Islamist threat.

Israel is, firstly, a nation state determined to live behind secure borders at a time when the fashion, particularly among radicals, is to dismantle nation states and erect transnational structures. Israel is also prepared, in order to defend its borders, to use military force, to pursue its enemies with all the legal and moral means at its disposal, and will not relegate the security of its people to second place behind the need to observe the sensitivities of outside judges, respond to the pious requirements of radical orthodoxy or make excuses for those who plot its destruction. Above all, in its desire to see its people safe and prosperous, Israel is not prepared to forfeit moral clarity to satisfy those who prefer moral relativism.

In each of these areas, the rest of the West is neither so resolute nor so certain. Israel's tragedy is that it stands so often alone. Our tragedy is that we will not stand with it, in embracing the values that will most effectively safeguard the West's future.

First, our security depends crucially on a recognition of the vital importance of maintaining the nation state, as ideal and reality. The nation state, as an organizing principle of political life, is central to Western thought and achievement. If political authority is to be exercised fairly, scrupulously and for the common good, then it has to be held accountable. The most important test of any democracy is the capacity to remove, and alter, rulers peacefully. The nation state is the political community that most effectively allows for the exercise of accountability.

Within a territory bound by common ties of language, history and culture, political leaders are able to make an appeal for shared sacrifice, whether it is asking for the taxation necessary to help the poorest or, at moments of greatest peril, calling on citizens to risk their lives to defend others. Without those common ties, appeals to sacrifice will not resonate, calls to forfeit individual freedom for the greater good will not receive a ready answering call. And without a common understanding of who we are, and why we stand together, political leaders cannot lead.

If we tire of a leadership, grow unwilling to accept a shared level of sacrifice, or perhaps believe that more is required of us all than our leadership is prepared to ask, then we need a mechanism to effect an alteration in course. The only effective mechanism that human nature and history have shown can allow such a change to take place without civil strife is the operation of liberal democracy. And the only political community in which liberal democracy has flourished – can flourish – is in a nation state. Because it is only within a nation state that leaders and citizens enjoy a sufficiently strong bond of fellow feeling, where the conversation between them can be made intelligible to both sides through shared experience, aspirations, language and assumptions.

Yet the nation state is under assault from forces determined to see it replaced, dismantled and supplanted. The radical impulses that have driven the Left since 1968 see in the nation state a source of repressive authority, an institution shaped by bourgeois power and tastes, a vehicle for tradition and reaction, an instrument of imperialism, a handmaiden of capitalism, a block on utopian schemes for the remaking of man and, above all, a symbol of the West, the oppressor.

The assault on the nation state takes many forms. Historians and cultural figures, from Linda Colley to Tom Nairn, seek to suggest that the nation state is an anachronism from which we need to escape. The European Union seeks to replace national systems of governance with a transnational union. Pressure groups, particularly those on the left, which fear they would not prevail within a democratic state structure, try to work through institutions that operate on a global level, at several removes from any semblance of accountability, such as the International Criminal Court or the World Health Organisation.

Hand in hand with the antipathy towards the nation state there exists a profound scepticism towards the principle that the West is allowed to use one of the essential tools of national independence – military force – in its own interests, and its own defence. As we saw during the debates before the Second Gulf War, the assumption has grown among many that military force can be deployed by democratic states only with the sanction of the United Nations. As far as the majority of the Labour Party was concerned, and certainly in the minds of most commentators, all military action without UN backing is automatically illegitimate.

On one level, the insistence that Britain could act only with UN backing is further proof of the declining faith in the capacity of the nation state to operate freely and independently. On a deeper level, it is remarkable that a democratic vote in the United Kingdom should not be considered truly legitimate unless it has been approved by a body that is, in itself, profoundly anti-democratic and that vests veto power in nations that are serial abusers of human rights. But, putting to one side those curiosities, the reluctance to support armed force deployed against Saddam Hussein is of a piece with a broader cultural antipathy to the use of military force in defence of British lives, interests and values. We have also seen that antipathy in the legal challenge to the use of lethal force against terrorists in Gibraltar and Northern Ireland, in the extension of new human rights legislation to cover army operations in the field, and in the decision to place the withdrawal of British army bases in Ulster on the same basis as terrorist decommissioning.

More powerfully, and importantly, we saw it and see it in the tone, tenor and intensity of the criticism directed towards ongoing Western military operations in Iraq and Afghanistan. There is a willingness to believe the worst, to question the legitimacy of any action, to doubt the wisdom of any intervention that goes beyond the prudent exercise of journalistic scepticism or political probing.

From the start of the intervention in Afghanistan the wisdom of committing forces was questioned on the basis of both legitimacy and justice. The West was warned that the exercise of removing the Taliban would be chancy and lengthy, exposing the citizens of the country to grave danger of starvation, displacement and trauma. It would be better, argued the Lib Dem Foreign Affairs Spokesman, Jenny Tonge, among others, to drop bread rather than bombs, to make our intervention purely humanitarian rather than military. In the event the operation to remove the Taliban took a matter of weeks, in the process the way was cleared to provide food, shelter and aid to the suffering, and Islamism received a crippling blow.

Central to Islamist thinking is the need to secure a defensible space in which Islamic law and practice can be imposed in a suitably totalitarian fashion. That territory acts as a processing centre for future jihadis, a template for other Muslims to emulate, and a military springboard for further conflict and conquest. Afghanistan provided that space for bin Laden and his Taliban allies. By denying them that territory, the West did not just deny them a base for terrorist operations, it deprived them of the essential prize of a land governed in accordance with pure Islamist principles to act as beacon, model and launchpad. Such a decisive blow would have been impossible without the use of military force, but before the war a swelling chorus of voices sought to deny that armed force could be of any use.

Significant as that chorus was before the war in Afghanistan, it was truly overwhelming before the war in Iraq and has become near-universal since. The wisdom of deploying military force in the first place was strenuously questioned. The war, it was promised, would result in the displacement of thousands, starvation, a refugee crisis, the destabilization of every neighbouring country (was that necessarily meant to be a bad thing?) and the rising of the Arab street in spontaneous armed revolt.

Within hours of operations beginning, any momentary delay in advance was attributed to the dogged 'patriotism' of Iraqi fighters who were undermining the clumsy Western juggernaut. After a matter of days Western tanks were on the outskirts of Baghdad, but the battle ahead, we were told, would be another Stalingrad. When, just a few days after that, Baghdad fell, then we were warned that Saddam himself would continue to be a rallying point for a 'patriotic' opposition that would restore him to power.

Of course, the conflict in Iraq has not been without errors, crimes and strategic misjudgements. But military force succeeded within a matter of weeks in removing a tyrant who had murdered millions over decades. It did not lead to mass displacement, a refugee crisis, the toppling of neighbouring regimes or an inflamed Arab street. We shall return in due course to the precise nature of the errors which have been made, and continue to be made, in that conflict. But at the heart of our misjudgement has been the application, not of too much force, but too little.

When military force has been applied with the rigour required to combat the insurgency, and to deprive it of space, resources and personnel, as in Fallujah, the effect has been beneficial. But the general reaction among Western commentators and politicians has been anguished horror of a kind that recalls nothing so much as the response to the Jenin police action. Yet, as with Jenin, the activity in Fallujah shows that it is only by retaining the option to use exemplary military force that terrorism can be deprived of the means of advance.

Israel has discovered, the hard way, that it needs the sense of common purpose and the willingness to accept shared sacrifice that strong nation-state structures provide in order to withstand terrorist assault. Israel has also learnt, through bitter struggle and many failed attempts to tread a gentler path, that only by retaining freedom of military action can security against terrorism be provided. And yet for these very reasons – its attachment to the nation state, its willingness to use force – it attracts particular opposition from the ranks of the radical Left. Those same forces seek to weaken the attachment the rest of the West has to the nation state, and the readiness others in the West have displayed to use military force in extremis. The consequences of this progressive weakening for our future security are profoundly troubling.

But these two principles are not the only values that Israel upholds, the radical Left opposes and the West needs to retain in the struggle against terror. There is a third, vital, element: the willingness to retain moral clarity at a time of moral relativism.

Ours is an age of many, and rapid, judgements. The question of what is 'in' or 'out', who is 'up' or 'down', which side has won a particular rhetorical exchange, or which force has momentum in any political contest, is always and endlessly being judged. But these judgements are carefully couched to avoid any taint of moral weight. The rightness or wrongness of any individual, cause, party or organization is seldom if ever pronounced on. It is simply their position relative to others, in a contest where relativity is all, that is judged. But the judgements that really matter are more and more difficult to make. In public, at least. The ability to pass a moral judgement, to declare a particular course of action superior, to uphold the values of a particular culture as more worthy of emulation, to declare without shame that what one knows is better than what others would wish to impose, is increasingly rare in the contemporary West.

In his penetrating book, *The Closing of the American Mind*, Professor Allan Bloom recorded the bewildered reaction of his undergraduates when asked to reflect on the superiority of one culture, one literary tradition, or one set of national political assumptions, over another. Such an activity was arrogant, presumptuous, illegitimate, potentially even racist. What Bloom recorded on the American campus in the Eighties has now become the dominant, default posture of most Western media and political conversation. The idea that the West's values are worth defending is considered eminently questionable. The proposition that they might in some way be intrinsically

superior to other cultures is scarcely allowable. Even the
notion that Western values might be better for those of us who
have grown up in the West is held to be a species of arrogance.
Who are we to say that our way is better? Isn't our judgement
as flawed, personal and subjective as any other? Why should it
be preferred?

The consequences of this truly radical version of equality,
which seeks to make each individual's response to any situation
as valid as any other, is the corrosion of any proper standard
of moral judgement. As we can see from our own media. This
collapse from moral relativism into moral equivalence has been
on particularly vivid display in the discussions around the War
on Terror.

Consider the case of Abu Ghraib prison. The revelation of
inhuman treatment in prisons run by the Americans put us,
according to many, on the same moral plane as Saddam. We
were both torturers. And thus the moral justification for the
war against Saddam evaporated. But such a judgement is
morally illiterate. In Saddam's Iraq, torture was an instrument
of social control and a source of private enjoyment for the
elite, torturers were promoted, and torture practised by the
most senior figures in the state. In the West, and in America,
torture is specifically outlawed, prisons are policed and statutes
tested to ensure that it does not take place and that those who
are discovered to break the rules are punished.

The scenes that occurred in Abu Ghraib were a stain on
America's record and a source of shame for the West. But they
were lapses from standards set, breaches of a carefully developed code, not deliberate state policy. Yet such is the moral relativism of our time that many in the media were determined to
make the events in Abu Ghraib the historic equivalent of
Saddam's policy of torture. Significant journalistic effort was
invested in establishing a link – which was, of course, never
found – between orders that flowed from the US President's

desk and the acts committed in Abu Ghraib. The appetite to find that link, the space and acclaim given to journalists attempting to make that link, and the willingness of political figures to insinuate such a linkage, is testament to a curious need. A significant section of Western opinion is not only ready to believe that the West is as bad as Ba'athist Iraq; it actively wants that to be so.

Consider also the debate around Saddam Hussein's trial. If one reviews the time allotted for discussion of the trial on, say BBC Radio Four's *Today* programme, or the space devoted to reporting it in, for example, the *Guardian*, the dominant theme has been the fairness or otherwise of the proceedings. Are Saddam's rights being respected? Or are we in the West once again trampling over human rights and due process? What is scarcely reported, and never given anything like the same prominence as the question of how we treat Saddam, is the mountain of evidence presented during the trial that attests to the sheer wickedness and brutality of Ba'athist Iraq, the brave testimony of those who suffered, and saw their relatives suffer, at Saddam's hands, the pitiable record of lives lost, massacres planned, atrocities executed. These become mere footnotes, noises off.

Why this curious inversion? Why so much discussion of the potential infringement of human rights in one man's trial and so little reporting of the massive, graphic destruction of human life at the same man's hands? Simple. In a world governed by moral relativism we must put ourselves on the same plane as a dictator. Our errors must be considered as worthy, if not more deserving, of condemnation as his.

An instant of moral clarity would allow us to see that the very fact that Saddam is in court, enjoying legal representation, a right to be heard and a platform to offer his own defence, rather than facing summary execution in the field, is evidence of extraordinary restraint and humanity on the part

of the West and our Iraqi allies. A second moment of moral
clarity would allow us to demand the proper publication, and
discussion, of the evidence against Saddam so that the world
could see judgement passed on a genocidal killer. A third display of moral clarity would involve us asking why so many in
the West are so anxious to find us the guilty party in any dispute; it would enable us to wonder what effect that posture has
in the ongoing battle we face against terror and tyranny.

But the space for moral clarity has been squeezed out by
the dominance of moral relativism. In a media world governed
by moral relativism the West is put in the dock for seeking to
restrain men found among our enemies on the field of battle.
But those same men never have to give a satisfactory answer as
to why they were standing alongside Islamist forces in the heart
of Taliban Afghanistan. The prison at Guantanamo Bay may
be a profoundly unsatisfactory place to hold enemy combat-
ants, but why is so much journalistic and political energy
deployed in criticizing it, when so little is deployed investigat-
ing why the British men who found themselves there were
themselves first found among the jihadists?

In the same spirit of moral relativism, the West's use of
'daisy-cutter' bombs or depleted uranium shells becomes a
cause célèbre, but the tactics of our enemies are scarcely
explored. How much space in the Western media has been
devoted to discussing the rules of jihad? How often have commentators reviewed the jihadist principle that all male unbe-
lievers beyond the age of puberty can be killed during war,
whether or not they belong to a formal military organization?
How often have Western newspapers reviewed, or even
revealed, the jihadist principle that no blame attaches to any
fighter who causes incidental deaths by using a weapon that
kills indiscriminately? When has the Western media made time
for a debate on the morality that governs jihadist treatment of
prisoners of war? The traditional Islamic view is that a Muslim

leader has the right to pursue any one of four courses of action when dealing with male POWs. He can 'cut the neck', enslave them, exchange them for money or a Muslim prisoner, and, finally, he can even free them. As we can see, when hostages such as Ken Bigley, Daniel Pearl and Nicholas Berg were beheaded, the cutting of their necks was not evidence of random savagery but proof of a strict adherence to the jihadist code of conduct. I do not, however, recall much media or political time being devoted to examining this particular rule of war, and asking what it reveals about the culture in question.

Furthermore, I could discuss the argument that we have no right, in the majesty of our Western arrogance, to 'impose' democracy. As if allowing people to choose their ruler, and indeed their form of government, can be understood, other than by twisting the English language out of all recognition, as an 'imposition'. I could ask on what basis life under an arbitrary, capricious and torture-addicted tyrant is morally superior to life under a ruler one can choose, and choose to remove, oneself.

The danger of moral relativism for any society faced by an external threat is profound and debilitating. Unless a society has the intellectual, and moral, resources to know what is worth preserving in its own culture then its values will not endure. Unless we retain the moral clarity to know that Western society, its freedoms and traditions, are worth celebrating, deserve to be emulated, and will benefit others by being adopted, then we will find them increasingly difficult to defend at a time of trial.

8

The Trojan Horse

Nowhere has moral clarity been more lacking in British state policy over the last ten to fifteen years than in our approach to the Islamist threat. Three particular errors have characterized our mistaken approach.

The first has been the willingness to extend a 'covenant of security' to known Islamist activists within the UK.

The second has been the determined playing down of the Islamist terror threat. Instead of recognizing the scale of the challenge mounted by political Islam, the British state persisted for years in believing that those who posed a direct danger to the country were a tiny renegade minority with no important connection to a broader ideological network.

The third has been the failure to scrutinize, monitor or check the actions, funding and operation of those committed to spreading the Islamist word within Britain.

All three errors are interconnected. They spring from a

basic failure of political intelligence, the inability properly to conceptualize the threat we face.

Some remedial action is finally being taken by the British state. The Prime Minister's own words in the aftermath of the 7/7 bombings indicated a promising direction of travel, at last, with a recognition that the threat we face is directly ideological. But since the Prime Minister's statement there have been worrying signs that progress towards developing the right policies has been fitful and compromised, and there is also evidence that some of the biggest problems we face continue to grow unaddressed.

The first error, the offer of a covenant of security, was a particularly shameful and short-sighted exercise in appeasement. The principle behind the covenant was simple. Islamist agitators were allowed safe haven within Britain, left free to preach, proselytize and plot on one condition: that they did not involve themselves in direct violent action within the UK. Thus Abu Hamza, Omar Bakri Mohammad[14] and Abu Qatada,[15] the Islamist who used Finsbury Park Mosque as a nursery for terrorists, the Islamist who set out to recruit jihadists for foreign operations, and the Islamist who, for a time, coordinated Al Qaeda operations across Europe, were left for years to pursue their chosen careers undisturbed.

Sometimes action might be contemplated against individual Islamists if foreign powers complained loudly enough. In the 1990s the Saudi authorities complained about the activities of Muhammad al-Massari, an exile from their country who was using Britain to coordinate an Islamist campaign against the Saudi royal family.[16] (There is a special irony in the Saudi authorities complaining about Islamist activists in Europe threatening civil order.) The British state explored options for deporting Mr al-Massari, but the judgement was made that under the 1951 UN Convention on Refugees he could not be removed because he did not pose a threat to

'British national security or public order'. So Mr al-Massari
stayed.

International treaties can, however, always be amended.
Derogations or exemptions can be sought by determined governments. And the law can always be changed. The law was
changed in 1998 with material effect in Mr al-Massari's case.
As a result of the Human Rights Act, which was passed into
law in that year, no individual can be deported if they are at
any risk of torture in the country to which they are returned.
The Saudi authorities offered the British courts a pledge that
no torture would be used against Mr al-Massari, but that
assurance was not considered good enough. So, protected even
more securely by British laws, and safe to operate at liberty
under the covenant of security, Mr al-Massari pursues his
political work unmolested. That work includes running a website that broadcasts, to edify the faithful, video footage of suicide bombings, including one from Iraq in which three British
soldiers were killed.[17] But since this clearly threatens neither
national security nor public order, Mr al-Massari can stay at
liberty.

As could Abu Hamza, for so many years. Until his arrest in
May 2004, Abu Hamza was free to preach, and practise, jihad
from British soil. As far back as October 1997, he publicly welcomed the terrorist murder of 58 European tourists in Egypt.
In 1999 he himself helped coordinate the kidnap of Western
tourists in Yemen, having spoken to the principal kidnapper by
satellite phone and dispatched his own recruits to the country
for jihad training. Hamza took over the effective running of
the Finsbury Park Mosque during this period, and while he
was in control it became a processing centre for Islamists who
went on to join terrorist activities abroad and was also a site for
weapons training. When Hamza was eventually arrested a
small armoury was uncovered on site. But Hamza was only
arrested in 2004, and only after the United States sought his

extradition in connection with plans to establish another terrorist training site in Oregon.

For seven years, during which time the Islamist terror threat was escalating, the British state did nothing worthwhile. For all the sophisticated chatter about savvy intelligence networks keeping a weather eye on Hamza, and using him as a means of monitoring Islamist undercurrents, the man was still left free to facilitate the advance of terrorism. Only the intervention of the US meant the courts had a chance to put him where he had long deserved to be.

Sadly, Hamza's brother in ideology, Omar Bakri Mohammad, is not in custody, but still at liberty, albeit in the Lebanon, having freely chosen to leave the United Kingdom after many happy years of jihadist activity within the UK. Omar Bakri Mohammad was among the first British Islamists to salute the 9/11 killers ('the Magnificent Nineteen')[18] and freely admitted that he recruited British Muslims for jihadist activity in Chechnya, Afghanistan and Jordan. Two of those linked to his recruitment drive were the young men Assif Muhammad Hanif and Omar Han Sharif. These two lads passed through the hands of his organization, Al-Muhajiroun, before they then took part in a suicide bombing attack against a bar in Tel Aviv in April 2003. Hanif's bomb detonated, killing three and wounding 65, but Sharif fled after failing to set off his bomb. His decomposed body was found floating off the Mediterranean coast almost two weeks later.[19]

Interestingly, Sharif's brother and sister were subsequently prosecuted under Section 38 of the Terrorism Act 2000, following suspicions that they knew of his intention to commit a terrorist offence. Sharif's brother had, in the days before the bombing, sent an e-mail warning him that 'difficult times might lie ahead' for his family and urging him to 'get rid of material you may consider problematic'. Sharif's sister had also sent a solicitous e-mail urging him to 'stay focused and determined' and reminding him that 'there is no time to be weak or emotional'.[20] Both were acquitted of any offence. It was, however, subsequently reported that Sharif's sister, a primary school teacher, had once told some of her charges that she was on Osama bin Laden's 'team'.[21]

One individual indisputably a member of the Osama bin Laden team was Abu Qatada, a radical cleric who operated as Al Qaeda's 'European ambassador'. Qatada helped groom Zaccarias Moussaoui, one of the 9/11 conspirators, and Richard Reid, the ex-convict and Muslim convert who tried to blow up an Air France plane with a bomb in his shoe. Qatada comes from the majority Palestinian community in the state of Jordan, but arrived in the United Kingdom in 1993 on a forged United Arab Emirates passport. He and his family applied for asylum in 1994 and were given permission to stay. He then applied for indefinite leave to remain. But no decision had been taken by the end of 2001, when he went on the run.

Qatada had absconded from his London home fearing arrest under new anti-terrorism laws. During his time in the UK he published propaganda in support of Algerian Islamist groups.[22] This activity was taking place at a time when a BBC TV presenter was being investigated by the police for saying disobliging things about the Welsh. But no one in authority within the British state thought to pursue Qatada for publishing material designed to incite terror.

Qatada was arrested in February 2001, after having been found in possession of over £150,000 in cash including £805 in an envelope marked 'for the mujahideen in Chechnya'.[23] It might have been thought odd that an individual who had been living exclusively on state benefits for himself and his family for seven years should have had so much ready cash to hand. It might have been considered appropriate, given that the gentleman's immigration status was in question, if the authorities had pursued not just what Abu Qatada was doing with that amount of money but what on earth he was doing at liberty in the UK. But no charges were brought.

Sometimes those who wish to defend the British state's handling of the Islamist threat argue that premature criminal prosecution of suspects can be counter-productive. It is better, they argue, to 'mark the card' of the individuals concerned, leave them at liberty, and then monitor their activities and contacts the better to build up a sophisticated intelligence picture of Islamist activity. It sounds a potentially sensible approach. Perhaps that is why Abu Qatada was left to operate as freely as he did – even at the cost of allowing him to send a shoe-bomber into a plane carrying hundreds of innocent travellers. But if Abu Qatada was being monitored by a sophisticated intelligence-gathering network then why was he able to abscond from his home in December 2001, evade the arresting authorities, and then remain at liberty until he was tracked down to a council house in South London in October 2002?

Intelligence officials are allowed to work behind a veil of secrecy to which other public servants are not entitled. The nature of intelligence operations requires discretion, confidence and secrecy. The contemporary media presumption in favour of the fullest possible disclosure at the earliest convenient moment is harmful enough, and positive folly in the case of intelligence. But nevertheless, in the case of Abu Qatada the public whom the intelligence services exist to protect deserve answers to some questions.

Why were men like Qatada, Hamza and Omar Bakri Mohammad left at liberty for so long? What evidence is there that they were subjected to serious scrutiny, or that their capacity to foment violence, from Yemen to Israel, from New York to Paris, was ever seriously interdicted? What was the rationale behind the covenant of security extended to them, and what was the evidence that any British citizen or interest was better protected by this process? How much time, space and money did the British state devote to monitoring the Islamist threat? How did that compare with foreign intelligence services, such as the French? And what representations did ministers and others receive from allies such as France about the threat posed by those Islamists we left at liberty?

More broadly, British citizens are entitled to ask questions of their policy-makers. How was it that men like these, some of whom entered the country illegally, were allowed to claim asylum, live off the generosity of the British taxpayer and then use British freedom, British money and British soil to plot mass-murder? And why did the laws you passed make it so difficult to do anything about them?

The precise nature of the legal problems we face in dealing with domestic terrorism will be considered in due course. But before leaving the question of the covenant of security, it is worth while to ask, does the spirit behind that approach still live on? Abu Hamza and Abu Qatada may, at last, be behind bars, and Omar Bakri Mohammad may, at least, be out of the country, but what about the treatment of others?

It was easy, and tempting, for some to regard Hamza, and even Omar Bakri Mohammad, as comic figures, Captain Hook and the Sheikh of Hate, intemperate ranters with raggle-taggle followers, bedsit revolutionaries with utopian fantasies of world domination. But we have learnt, the hard way, that they were capable of moving men to violence and coordinating vicious campaigns of terror. And history should have reminded us that intemperate ranters with raggle-taggle followers whom sophisticates find it easy to mock can, if left unchecked, find themselves in a position to unleash truly terrible violence. That is certainly the lesson of the careers of Mussolini, Hitler, Khomeini and Kim Il Sung.

So when we are tempted to smile at the outrageous claims made by the likes of Anjem Choudray on *Newsnight* when this eccentric preacher claims England for Allah, we should check ourselves. This is the man chosen by his fellow Islamists to take up where Hamza and Omar Bakri Mohammad left off.[24] An evangelist for totalitarianism and an advocate of violence. For years he has been happily at liberty, free to recruit, exploiting the airwaves, ready to strike. A figure of fun? I think we know who has the last laugh.

The same authorities who allowed the likes of Choudray[25] to remain at liberty also allowed the recent pro-terrorist demonstrations outside the Danish Embassy in London. Why were individuals allowed to march through Central London praising suicide bombers, saluting terrorism and warning the West that divine retribution was on the way? Why were placards carried proudly through our streets warning Britain's Jewish community to prepare for the 'real' holocaust? Why were no arrests carried out that day? Why were the only people moved on and suppressed by the police those who felt they had to object to the celebration of terrorism in their own country?

We have been assured that the absence of arrests was due to 'smart policing' that puts vital intelligence-gathering ahead of the clumsy old arrest, prosecute and jail approach to law enforcement. But what is the material difference between the approach behind 'smart policing' and the failed philosophy behind the 'covenant of security'? Don't both involve giving the enemies of the West the space to operate freely while we delude ourselves that we have them under observation? Haven't we learnt that the failure to act does not just allow Islamists time and space to operate but also, crucially, reinforces their impression of our weakness? Once again, and not for the last time, our culture is incapable of asserting itself in defence of liberal values. Islamists draw strength and take heart from what they see as our terminal irresolution.

The Islamists so encouraged are not restricted only to the high-profile few whom the British state claims to keep under observation and who are flagrant enough to proclaim their open sympathy for terrorism in the public square. Those Muslims who are open in their determination to see jihad prosecuted are often depicted as not just a small minority but a tiny, unrepresentative, renegade minority, a faction whose interpretation of their faith, and its requirements, is utterly at odds with the overwhelming majority of believers. It is reassuring to imagine that the problem we face is restricted to a very small group of individuals who are already isolated within the larger Muslim community and whom, with application, it will be easy to identify and deal with, without having to engage on any broader front.

But however reassuring it may be to work on that basis, it would be fatally misconceived. Just as the Nazi Brownshirts were simply the visible, aggressive, street expression of a wider radical conservative movement in Weimar Germany, and the Bolsheviks in Tsarist Russia were just the spearhead for a wider movement of social discontent, so those jihadists who make the case for violent action now are the militant vanguard of a wider movement. There are many Muslims, across the globe, within Europe and in Britain, who share the basic ideological assumptions behind the jihadist worldview.

The thinkers who inspire the most energetic Islamist activists, the figures such as al-Banna, Qutb and Mawdudi, whose ideas we explored at the beginning, are followed and revered by many millions beyond those prepared to countenance the use of violence now. The Islamist belief system, the ideology of political Islam, has a hold over a great many individuals and organizations that claim to speak for British and European Muslims. The belief that Islamic law should govern human relations, that Western notions of equality between the sexes are an offence against nature, that sovereignty belongs to Allah alone, that Western secular society is decadent and Islam the future, is shared by a broad spectrum of Muslim opinion. At one end of this spectrum are those so determined to bring about Islam's advance that they seek to prosecute jihad with all the force they can muster. But these individuals, while they may form a minority in their willingness to contemplate such direct action now, are part of a much broader network of Muslims whose conception of the future, and attachment to politicized Islam, places them at odds with the values of the liberal West.

In that respect the fight against Islamist terrorism cannot be restricted to a police action against isolated individuals or small groups, although it would certainly be reassuring to see such efforts effectively prosecuted. A much broader effort is required to tackle, at root, the ideology of Islamism that has bewitched so many minds. It is a point that has not been lost on the Prime Minister. Speaking after the 7/7 bombings and explicitly rejecting the claims made by moral relativists that the attacks were somehow 'inspired', 'justified' or 'explained' by the war in Iraq, Mr Blair made clear the scale of the challenge:

> We will start to beat this when we stand up and confront the ideology of this evil. Not just the methods but the ideas. When we actually have people going into the [Muslim] communities here in this country and elsewhere and saying I am sorry, we are not having any of this nonsense about it is to do with what the British are doing in Iraq or Afghanistan, or support for Israel, or support for America, or any of the rest of it. It is nonsense, and we have got to confront it as that. And when we confront it as that, then we will start to beat it. And we are not going to deal with this problem, with the roots as deep as they are, until we confront these people at every single level. And not just their methods, but their ideas.

But who are these people? And where do they propagate their ideas? The answers are, in many respects, uncomfortable. According to the polls, a sizeable minority of Britain's 1.8 million Muslims hold rejectionist Islamist views:

46 per cent consider themselves Muslim first and British second.

31 per cent believe that Western society is decadent and immoral, and that Muslims should bring it to an end by peaceful means.

24 per cent sympathize with the 'feelings and motives' of the bombers.

26 per cent *do not* think that the ideas that led the bombers to carry out their attacks were 'poisonous and perverted'.

45 per cent *do not* think that Muslim clerics who preach that violence against the West can be justified are out of touch with mainstream Muslim opinion.

40 per cent wish to see sharia law implemented in the UK.

A recent Populus poll of British Muslims published in *The Times* displayed some more disturbing trends.

A majority regard the Jewish community and its links to Israel with suspicion. More than half think both that it is right to boycott Holocaust Memorial Day and that the Jewish community has too much influence over British foreign policy. Nearly two fifths (37 per cent) believe that the Jewish community in Britain is a legitimate target 'as part of the ongoing struggle for justice in the Middle East'. Moreover, only 52 per cent think that the state of Israel has the right to exist, with 30 per cent disagreeing – a big minority. One in six of all Muslims questioned thinks suicide bombings can sometimes be justified in Israel, though many fewer (7 per cent) say the same about Britain. This is broadly comparable to the number justifying suicide attacks in ICM and YouGov polls of British Muslims after the 7 July attacks.

However, according to Populus, 12 per cent of 18- to 24-year-old Muslims believe that suicide bombings can be justified here, while 21 per cent approve of them in Israel. A fifth of all

Muslims, and a quarter of men, say suicide attacks against the military can be justified, though only 7 per cent say this about civilians. Other highlights of the poll include the revelation that 46 per cent of Muslims believe that Jews are 'in league with the Freemasons to control the media and politics'.

These views were not developed in a vacuum. They reflect the influence of organized work by those sympathetic to an Islamist agenda within the United Kingdom.

The British government has indicated that it is prepared to proscribe certain organizations it considers responsible for glorifying terror, specifically Hizb ut-Tehrir, the offshoot of the Muslim Brotherhood whose philosophy was referred to earlier, and the organization that seeks to pick up the work embarked on by Omar Bakri Mohammad.

However, as the *New Statesman*'s Political Editor Martin Bright has reported, the government has been reluctant to move with unity and speed against these organizations. And even if the government did succeed in successfully proscribing these organizations it would only be tackling two of the most flagrant manifestations of UK support for Islamism. There is powerful evidence that the attitudes that underpin support for political Islam exist in a form far more widespread than membership of these organizations. And if the government is going to make good on the Prime Minister's pledge to tackle the 'ideas' behind Islamist activity then a much more ambitious programme of ideological work is required. A range of groups need to be taken on ideologically.

One of the most influential Muslim groups in Britain is the Muslim Association of Britain. The MAB played a key part in the Stop the War Coalition and helped organize the rally against the war in Iraq at which the then Liberal Democrat leader Charles Kennedy spoke in 2003. The MAB also organized a rally in London in February 2006, following the anti-free speech and pro-terror protests that took place outside the

Danish Embassy. The MAB claimed that its rally, also intended to signal disapproval of Danish cartoonists, would nevertheless show a more moderate and responsible face of Islam. The Liberal Democrat front-bencher Sarah Teather spoke at the gathering.

But the Muslim Association of Britain is not a 'moderate' movement.[26] It is the UK branch of the Muslim Brotherhood, the organization created by Islamism's founding father, Hassan al-Banna. The Brotherhood's Palestinian branch is, of course, Hamas. The MAB was responsible for engineering an invitation for Sheikh Yusuf al-Qaradawi to come to the United Kingdom in 2004. Qaradawi is on record as favouring wife-beating,[27] physical punishment for the crime of homosexuality,[28] and 'martyrdom' (suicide bombing) operations against Israeli civilians.

The Sheikh has argued that 'We must all realize that the Israeli society is a military society – men and women. We cannot describe the society as civilian ... they are not civilians or innocent.' He has also supported the use of child suicide bombers. During a TV debate in the Gulf – according to BBC monitoring – he said: 'The Israelis might have nuclear bombs but we have the children bomb and these human bombs must continue until liberation.'

Sheikh Qaradawi has, incidentally, also described the Islamist insurgency in Iraq as 'valiant', and lest that be considered a detached acknowledgement of their physical courage, he is also, according to the Lebanese National News Agency website, reported to have said: 'We call for material, military and human support ... the Muslims want the scholars to show the Arab and Muslim person's duty is towards this cause.' As Anthony Browne of *The Times* has pointed out, the Sheikh is also editor-in-chief of Islamonline.net, which insists that it is the duty of Muslims to 'achieve supremacy on earth and put their enemies to rout' and asserts that 'the means for doing so is taking up arms in addition to preparation, financing and planning strategies'.

As well as venerating the Sheikh the MAB provides space on its own website for adoring accounts of the lives and achievements of Islamism's other principal theoreticians, including al-Banna and Sayyid Qutb. The MAB not only respects Islamist theory, it respects Islamist practice.

The MAB's spokesman, Dr Azzam al-Tamimi, explained his support for Hamas in an interview with the BBC's Tim Sebastian on News 24's *HARDtalk* in November 2004. Dr Tamimi declined to condemn suicide bombings as murder, preferring instead to describe them as part of a 'struggle'.

Dr Tamimi's record, statements and beliefs were explored in the House of Commons by the Labour MP Louise Ellman in 2003. Mrs Ellman quoted from a number of Mr Tamimi's speeches, including one in Vienna in which he reportedly said that Israel would be destroyed and replaced by an Islamic state, and that the Jews should 'sail on the sea in ships back to where they came from and all drown in it'. Addressing a Palestinian Solidarity rally in Westminster last year, Mr Tamimi allegedly said: 'Listen, Israel and Jews around the world, unless you change there is no future for you.'

In response to Mrs Ellman's comments Dr Tamimi defended his position by arguing that: 'As a Muslim, martyrdom is an integral part of Islamic theology and these young men from the Islamic perspective are not committing suicide.' He added: 'What they are doing is that they are turning themselves as an act of sacrifice into bombs because this is the only way to stop Israel from attacking Palestinians.'

The Muslim Association of Britain is not the only organization that aspires to speak for British Muslims whose leading figures have also shown sympathy for Hamas and its campaign of terror. The Muslim Council of Britain is perhaps the single most influential organization that seeks to represent the inter-

ests of British Muslims. Its Secretary-General is Sir Iqbal
Sacranie, the gentleman who once argued that death was 'perhaps too easy' for Salman Rushdie. In 2004 Iqbal Sacranie
attended a memorial service at Regent's Park Mosque for
Sheikh Ahmed Yassin, the former spiritual leader of Hamas.[29]
The MCB itself paid tribute to Sheikh Yassin by describing the
terrorist ideologue as a 'noted Islamic scholar'.

Sheikh Yassin is not the only ideologue of terror to whom
the MCB has paid its respects. The MCB has also, like its affil-
iate the MAB, offered tributes to the leader of the Muslim
Brotherhood, Sheikh Qaradawi, arguing that he has been 'a
distinguished Muslim scholar ... a voice of reason and understanding'.[30] We should remember that this is the man who has
been reported as calling for material aid to be offered to the
insurgents in Iraq who are currently targeting British troops.

Sir Iqbal Sacranie's organization may be happy to offer
kind words for Sheikhs Yassin and Qaradawi, but it has shown
a cold shoulder to Britain's Jews. Sir Iqbal and his media
spokesman Inayat Bunglawala have both, pointedly, declined
to attend the United Kingdom's Holocaust Memorial Day
commemorations.[31] Mr Bunglawala, who has recently been
asked to help the Home Office combat Islamist extremism, has
an interesting record himself. In 1993 he wrote a letter to
Private Eye praising the Islamist cleric Sheikh Omar Abdul
Rahman as 'courageous'. One month later the Sheikh attempted
to blow up the World Trade Center. Following the Sheikh's
arrest Mr Bunglawala claimed the cleric had only been
detained because he had been 'calling on Muslims to fulfil their
duty to Allah and to fight against oppression and oppressors
everywhere'.

Mr Bunglawala is also on record as having told the
Financial Times that Osama bin Laden was 'a freedom fighter.
He was regarded in large sections of the Muslim world before
2001 as a freedom fighter for what he had done in

Afghanistan.' He subsequently disowned those remarks, but he has nevertheless displayed a curious way of finding fault with the British media. One offence in particular has irked him: what he perceives to be its pro-Israel bias. Writing in a Muslim youth magazine in 1992 he thought it necessary to point out that: 'The chairman of Carlton Communications is Michael Green of the Tribe of Judah. He has joined an elite club whose members include fellow Jews Michael Grade [then the chief executive of Channel 4 and now BBC chairman] and Alan Yentob [BBC2 controller and friend of Salman Rushdie].'[32]

The prominent roles played by Sir Iqbal and Mr Bunglawala need to be seen in context. The MCB aspires to act as an umbrella organization for more than 400 affiliated groups, and within such a broad family there will inevitably be divergences. But for many British Muslims the MCB is not broad, or representative enough. They see it as the voice of those British Muslims whose theology is uncompromisingly conservative and their politics dangerously radical. Many leaders of Britain's Sufi community, which is undoubtedly more mainstream in its representation of UK's Muslims, have felt moved to set up their own organization, the British Muslim Forum, to ensure that there is a voice for the moderate majority. The BMF and its supporters have been disturbed by the influence the MCB and its even more radical affiliates such as the MAB exercise in political and media circles. They are concerned by the ideological lineage behind the MCB.

As the BBC's John Ware pointed out in his groundbreaking *Panorama* investigation into the MCB, 'A Question of Leadership', broadcast in August 2005, the Council has drawn intellectual nourishment from some worrying sources. One of the most important and influential affiliates of the MCB is the Islamic Foundation in Leicester. The Foundation was set up in the UK in 1974 and was instrumental in creating the MCB. The Foundation exists to support and propagate the beliefs of

the Islamist ideologue Abul Ala Mawdudi. The Chairman and
Rector of the Foundation, Professor Khurshid Ahmad, is also
Vice-President of the party Mawdudi founded in Pakistan, the
Jamaat-i-Islami.

Mawdudi's thought, as was outlined at the beginning of
this book, is a key influence on Islamists and jihadis across the
globe. Like Hassan al-Banna and Sayyid Qutb, Mawdudi
argued that Islam was not just a system of 'some beliefs,
prayers and rituals' but a total way of life that should guide
every element of an individual's life and every aspect of their
society and political culture. Muslims should seek to see sharia
law respected and implemented wherever they lived and, in due
course, all across the globe. Progress towards Islamicizing the
whole world demanded a rejection of the West, whose values
would lead only to decadence, and the embrace of jihad.
Mawdudi specifically argued in his work *Jihad in Islam* that
Islam was a 'revolutionary concept and ideology which seeks
to change and revolutionize the world social order and reshape
it according to its own concept and ideals'.

When questioned by John Ware about the relevance of
Mawdudi's revolutionary message for British Muslims, Sir
Iqbal Sacranie offered the Islamist ideologue an endorsement
every bit as generous as those his organization has extended to
Sheikhs Yassin and Qaradawi:

> Mawdudi is a renowned scholar. I have read many of his
> books and I believe he is one of the scholars that I certainly
> feel is an inspiration to many of us. Institutions like the
> Islamic Foundation are playing a very important role and we
> are proud to have them as our affiliates.

The Islamic Foundation is very far from being the only
Islamist organization at work within the UK whose activities
the MCB has saluted. Hizb ut-Tehrir is one of the organizations whose Islamist credentials are sufficiently transparent for

the UK government to wish to proscribe it,[33] as the German government has. HuT was instrumental in the campaign to compel Denbigh High School in Luton to allow one of its pupils, Shabina Begum, to flout the rules on acceptable dress by wearing the jilbab, a restrictive form of dress for women favoured by fundamentalists. Although there is no Koranic injunction or scriptural authority that requires the wearing of the jilbab, and although Denbigh High School has a fully worked-out uniform policy developed in consultation with the local Muslim community, HuT was determined to fight Ms Begum's case through every court in the land. For Islamists the fight was symbolic – would a Western nation be strong enough to defend the idea of secular space and equal rights or could the public square be colonized for an idealized, politicized and culturally specific version of Islam? It was understandable the HuT should celebrate a temporary victory in the courts. What was, perhaps, and then again perhaps not, more surprising was the welcome given to HuT's victory by the MCB. According to Inayat Bunglawala, it was a 'very important ruling, sending a very clear signal that personal freedoms and right to practise one's faith ought to be respected'.[34]

In the struggle against extremism the British state has not only failed to deal effectively with those openly committed to jihad, it has also failed to tackle the underlying ideological currents that favour Islamism. Organizations such as the MAB and MCB are rarely challenged, and certainly not publicly by the government or its agencies. Institutions like the Islamic Foundation, and the message they propagate, are never properly engaged.[35]

For moderate Muslims the picture is, inevitably, dispiriting. They see how the most religiously conservative and politically provocative groupings enjoy the lion's share of political and media attention and they inevitably wonder how serious the British state and leaders of UK opinion are about countering extremism. How can they convince young men within their community that the path of moderation brings respect and a voice in the nation's deliberations when the most influential voices are seen to belong to those with radical agendas? In Islamist circles a complementary message is absorbed. The British state does not have the wit, or perhaps the courage, to face down the advocates of political Islam and is happy to either work with them, or give them space to advance their own agenda, appropriately respected and suitably indulged. Islamists in Britain scent weakness. Despite the Prime Minister's strong rhetoric, they discern no stomach for the necessarily prolonged and difficult task of facing them down. Just as Islamists abroad believe the West lacks the stamina or resolution to resist for long, so Islamists within the UK believe the momentum is with them. Islam's Leninists have drawn the bayonet, probed, and found mush.

Proof of the institutional weakness of the British state when it comes to dealing with Islamism and its supporters came directly in the aftermath of the 7/7 bombings. At the Prime Minister's behest the Home Office established a series of working groups to tackle the threat of Islamic extremism. Prominent British Muslims were appointed to these groups. Some of them, like the Sufi businessman Haris Rafiq and the former Deputy Chairman of the CRE Khurshid Ahmad, are exemplary moderate figures: pious Muslims and British patriots committed to peace and cultural harmony. One might have expected that these would have been the precise criteria that the Home Office would have set for membership.

Far from it. As well as Inayat Bunglawala from the MCB a variety of individuals were appointed whose past statements or current affiliations made them very curious conscripts in the struggle against extremism. Among those appointed was Mr Ahmad Thomson, a Zimbabwe-born barrister and convert to Islam who has argued in the past that Hitler was supported by

Zionist financiers and that it is the duty of Muslims to want to live in an Islamic state. Another figure appointed was Ibrahim Hewitt,[36] who sits on the ruling council of Respect, the political party founded by George Galloway, which fuses together the Trotskyist SWP and the Islamist Muslim Association of Britain. Mr Hewitt also helps run the charity Interpal along with Dr Azzam al-Tamimi and Anas al-Tikriti from the MAB. Like Sir Iqbal Sacranie and Inayat Bunglawala, Mr Hewitt takes issue with Holocaust Memorial Day.

Also invited to advise the government in its efforts to tackle extremism was Dr Tariq Ramadan, the grandson of Hassan al-Banna, founder of the Muslim Brotherhood. Dr Ramadan is not, of course, obliged to follow in the footsteps of his fore-bears. But he gives it a pretty good try. Asked by the Italian magazine *Panorama* about the killing of civilians, Ramadan said: 'In Palestine, Iraq, Chechnya, there is a situation of oppression, repression and dictatorship. It is legitimate for Muslims to resist fascism that kills the innocent.' Asked about attacks on US forces in Iraq, Professor Ramadan responded: 'Iraq was colonized by the Americans. The resistance against the army is just.'[37]

Professor Ramadan has been characterized as a moderate because he has said that he 'agrees with integration' of Muslims in the West. But he has also insisted that 'we [Muslims] are the ones who are going to decide the content'. Bernard Kouchner, the French Socialist and former health minister, has described Ramadan as 'absolutely a kook with no historical memory' and 'a dangerous man'. Kouchner has also argued that: 'The way he denounced some Jewish intellectuals is close to anti-Semitism.' And yet Tariq Ramadan, banned from America and France, is fellow of an Oxford college, and a man the British government believes perfectly equipped to help it counter extremism.

Given the presence of these, and of others with a similar

perspective, on the Home Office's working groups, it should not be surprising that the conclusions reached found fault not so much within Islam as within the British state, its institutions, allies and foreign policy. I have had the opportunity to question some of those involved with the working groups' operation and I know that there is doubt and disquiet at the highest level about their membership and conclusions.* Among a series of policy proposals that give rise to concern, three were specifically identified.

The group tasked with formulating policies to engage with young people recommended allocating £100,000 of taxpayers' money to a programme, one of whose lead agencies would be the Federation of Student Islamic Societies (FOSIS). FOSIS's constituent societies have been among those leading campaigns for the boycott of Israeli goods on Britain's campuses. FOSIS's own website attacks Tony Blair for characterizing those who wish to establish a worldwide Islamic Caliphate as extremist. And it defends, among others, Tariq Ramadan, Azzam al-Tamimi and Sheikh Yusuf Qaradawi from the charge of extremism. Is giving this organization tens of thousands of pounds of public money really the most effective way of leading young people away from radical Islam?

The Federation of Student Islamic Societies is not the only group asked to fight extremism that appears to deny that it's a problem. The Home Office's Security and Policing Working Group argued that the phrase 'Islamic extremism' was itself 'offensive'. This working group then set out to consider not the policing of our streets, nor the policing of extremist activities, but the policing of our language. The government and the Muslim community were urged to agree on 'Guidelines on appropriate language, and appropriate Procedures to ensure

---

* I am particularly grateful to Garvan Walshe and Dean Godson for assisting me in close study of the working group's operations and recommendations.

that these Guidelines are followed'. Given that the Group felt references to Islamic extremism were offensive, what other expressions might they wish to see deemed inappropriate and placed outside the acceptable Guidelines?

The Security and Policing Working Group's recommendation was not, however, the only proposal put to the Home Office that would have closed down debate. The Working Group's report – which was actually commissioned to come up with ideas to put Islamist extremists on the defensive – instead puts the free Press in the dock. The report recommended establishing a Unit at the Department of Culture Media and Sport to 'encourage a more balanced representation of Islam and Muslims in the British media, (popular) culture and sports industries'. In other words, the best way to tackle extremism is to ensure that the Press doesn't continuously draw attention to it. This policy suggestion was just one of several attempts to set up a government body to control public thought and discussion.

These three recommendations, like so much of the report, betrayed a consistent reluctance to confront the reality of Islamist influence and operation in the UK. In so far as extremism was acknowledged as a danger it was attributed to the foreign policy of Blair and Bush. And in so far as remedial action was required it seemed, again and again, to consist of more public money going to exclusively Islamic bodies that would be empowered to provide more Islamic solutions, in accordance with appropriate Islamic principles.

Again, in conversation with moderate Muslims, the folly of such a strategy is repeatedly underlined. Mainstream Muslims, especially those from the majority Sufi community, wish to participate fully in the life of our nation as equal citizens. Their Islamic faith is an important, integral part of their identity, but they do not wish it to be the exclusive route through which they relate to the rest of Britain.

But the approach of organizations such as the MAB and MCB – an approach reinforced by the Working Group's Report on Combating Extremism – is to Islamicize every issue with which Muslims come into contact. Public money should be funnelled through groups that are Islamic in character, faith and identity. Campaigning energy should be directed towards issues that heighten a sense of transnational Muslim identity and feed a sense of common Muslim grievance rather than bringing real and measurable improvements to individual British citizens. So the MCB and MAB campaign on issues such as Palestine, Iraq and Chechnya instead of women's access to higher education, improved childcare and employment opportunities. The MCB and MAB champion the rights of terrorist suspects in Guantanamo Bay and individuals who wish to dress in a fundamentalist fashion and then complain that Muslim identity is viewed through the prism of the War on Terror and refracted by perceptions of religious extremism.

The success of the MCB, MAB and their allies in dominating the public debate, shaping public policy and driving the media conversation has been profoundly damaging for relations between Muslim Britons and their fellow citizens. A narrow version of Islam has been privileged, theological conservatism reinforced, and political radicalism given room to advance. A rising generation has been encouraged by those Muslims most prominent in public life to put their Islamic identity ahead of their British citizenship. That generation will have heard the Muslims most fêted by government and most listened to by the media pay tribute to terrorist leaders and fundamentalist ideologues as figures worthy of respect. That generation will also have had its sense of grievance nurtured even as its sense of separateness has been reinforced. For Islamists and their allies, it has been a golden prospect. And while the prospect of a brighter dawn beckons for them, there is the complementary comfort of knowing that so many of the institutions that support and facilitate their advance can continue to operate unmolested in the shadows.

The British state has failed in extending a covenant of security to some of Islamism's most aggressive evangelists. It has failed to recognize the nature of the broad front on which Islamism is advancing. But it has also, signally, failed to keep any effective watch on the external financial and cultural support that has been given to Islamism within the UK. The Chancellor of the Exchequer, Gordon Brown, recently boasted about the British state's energetic determination to pursue terrorist money-laundering, and his zeal in that regard does him credit. But criminally obtained cash for terrorist operations is only one of the financial flows the British state should be concerned about.

One of the broadest avenues of Islamist advance across the globe comes through the Saudi funding of fundamentalist religious instruction and practice. The relationship between the Saudi ruling family and the aggressively intolerant Wahhabi strain of Islam has been well documented. The Wahhabi foundations of the Saudi state mean that Christian practice is outlawed in the Desert Kingdom and women face a number of penal restrictions on their liberty, which govern how they may dress, drive, work and walk. But while Saudi elites seek to retain the approval of the Islamist clerics who have fashioned the law of the land by maintaining a regime of public sharia, those same elites are found wanting in two material areas. First, as Osama bin Laden has pointed out, the Saudis have relied on the presence of American troops on their soil to bolster their rule, not least by protecting them in the past from Saddam's Iraq. By allowing infidel soldiers to occupy the land of Mecca and Medina, the site of Mohammad's revelation, the Saudi elites are held to be gravely compromising the purity of their rule. Westoxification in the eyes of the Islamists, of course, goes further than just accommodating American troops. The ostentatious wealth of Saudi elites and their poorly disguised enjoyment of Western luxuries is a second, and grievous, act of apostasy that can be charged to their account.

In order to buy compliance from as many within Wahhabi and Islamist circles as possible, Saudi elites have reached a curious compact. They hope to divert attention from their own errors, and to buy acquiescence in their continued rule, by paying for the spread of Islamist doctrine abroad. So Saudi leaders organize telethons to raise money for Islamist terror campaigns against Israel. Saudi money goes to fund the publication, and distribution, of Islamist texts and commentaries. Saudi cash supports the activities of Islamist clerics and evangelists across the globe. And Saudi billions fund the operations of mosques across the globe in which the faithful, whatever their original orientation or cultural background, are led into a fundamentalist reading of their faith.

The extent of Saudi funding of Islamist activity has been powerfully recorded in Dore Gold's book *Hatred's Kingdom*, but the extent of Saudi, and indeed other, funding of Islamist activity within the UK has eluded any systematic British state surveillance.

We do know that the Saudis are funders of the London Central Mosque in Regent's Park and the East London Mosque. It is significant, in that regard, that it was the Regent's Park Mosque that recently hosted the memorial service for Hamas leader Sheikh Yassin and the East London Mosque that recently entertained as its guest of honour a Saudi cleric, Sheikh Abdur-Rahman al-Sudais, who has described Jews as 'pigs and monkeys', and Hindus as 'idol worshippers' and 'enemies of Islam' to whom it would be wrong to 'talk sweetly'.[38]

Saudi funding is clearly linked, at the very least, to leaving an open door to Islamist and extremist influence. But while British law and practice generally requires effective disclosure of how charitable and voluntary organizations are funded, the

British state does not have an up-to-date and accurate record of which mosques, madrassas and other religious establishments receive funding from which sources, let alone what is taught and disseminated within them – neither the content of sermons, nor the nature of instruction offered to the young, nor the attitudes inculcated towards other faiths. No effective means of examining what is going on at the heart of our society exists, as yet. Some former Islamists, such as Dr Ghayasuddin Siddiqui, of the Muslim Institute, have suggested creating a formal mechanism to provide institutional oversight of activity within mosques. Both the Prime Minister and the Leader of the Opposition have acknowledged that further action needs to be taken. But still we wait.

And while we have waited, the Islamists have not been idle. Over the early months of 2006 their cause received a significant boost from the controversy surrounding the publication of cartoons in Denmark depicting Muhammad. The decision by the Danish newspaper *Jyllands Posten* to publish a series of cartoons featuring the prophet was inspired by the difficulties faced by the publisher of a children's book in finding an appropriate illustration of the prophet Mohammad to accompany the text. The cartoons were intended to draw attention to what was considered a restriction on free expression – which they certainly did. In a manner that none of those involved in the original commissioning process could have quite envisaged.

After an appreciable delay, the publication of the cartoons inspired a reaction of remarkable ferocity and passion. Danish embassies were attacked and set on fire. Scandinavian citizens in the Middle East faced physical harassment. Street riots across the Islamic world were accompanied by violence and, in some cases, ended in death. Protesters took to the streets of London promising terrorist retribution.

Some of this reaction was the spontaneous and heartfelt expression of deep hurt at personal faith mocked. It should, however, be noted that the question of whether, or how, Mohammad may be depicted has been a subject of debate within the Islamic world rather than a settled issue. It should also be remembered that the original injunction against the reproduction of his image was intended to prevent idolatry – elevating the prophet's likeness to an inappropriate status and extending undue reverence to images. In that light, the actions of many of the protesters can be seen as exhibiting the very fault, of sin, or idolatry about which they claimed to be concerned.

But if some protesters were sincere and spontaneous, albeit potentially misguided, there were also darker forces at work.

The initial publication of the cartoons in the autumn of 2005 passed without significant comment, or outrage. This was much to the chagrin of a group of Danish Islamists who set out to provoke as militant a response as possible. They toured the Middle East seeking to incite anger at the cartoons. But perhaps they feared that the images concerned were insufficiently provocative for mainstream Muslims to be moved to violence, so the Danish Islamists interpolated other disturbing images into the portfolio of cartoons. It was only after these images received widespread circulation that the reaction sought by the Islamists was secured.[39]

The scenes of angry and rioting young men across the Middle East led the news bulletins for several days, during which the Danish Embassy in Syria came under assault and Danish flags were burnt in the streets of Saudi Arabia. It should be noted that Syria is a police state in which no one is allowed to riot, without official sanction, if they value their life and liberty. And the idea that any official property or foreign residence in Damascus could be 'stormed' without clear direction from above stretches credulity.

Also, as far as the flags are concerned, is it really credible that in the impoverished back streets of the Arab Middle East,

Danish flags are as common as keffiyahs and Korans? Are we expected to believe that every Arab family keeps in store a collection of EU flags ready to be incinerated the next time a Western nation is foolish enough to run the wrong sort of cartoons? Given the deliberate process by which Denmark's Islamists sought to provoke uproar by circulating the cartoons alongside slyly manufactured and extravagantly offensive images, what other steps do we think they took? Might the ready availability of Danish flags on Arab streets have a lot more to do with choreographed political action than with spontaneous personal affront?

Wherever the Danish flags came from, those burning them knew what they wanted to see from Europe – evidence of the white flag being waved in return. And that came soon enough. The Islamists protesting at these cartoons were trying simultaneously to restrict free speech, dictate the terms on which the West treated Islam, and test the West's resolution in the face of intimidation. On all three fronts they scored a resounding victory.

Consider first the question of publication or, more pertinently, republication of the cartoons. It may well have been silly, or offensive, to publish the cartoons in the first place. They weren't that illuminating. Or even that witty. But as soon as an organized group of religious totalitarians argued that the cartoons must not be published then the case for publication actually became imperative. Newspaper and magazine readers had a right to see what all the fuss was about. Just what sort of image was it that would drive Islamists to coordinate a global campaign of violence and intimidation? More importantly, any refusal to show the cartoons was going to be interpreted, rightly, by the religious totalitarians as a timorous surrender to their threats.

It was only by publishing the cartoons that the British media could have shown that they would not have the content of their publications dictated by Islamist censorship. But not a single British newspaper dared to publish the cartoons. And thus we advertised our weakness to the world.

In that context, a word of praise should go to those media outlets, including *Die Welt* in Germany, that did dare to publish. It is a conceit of the British Press that we as a nation, and they as newspapers, are much more robust than our European neighbours. As we can see from this episode, and indeed from how the French, for example, treat their terrorist suspects, we have a lot to learn.

The self-censorship that the British media imposed over the publication of the cartoons was only one of a number of genuflections to Islamist concerns at this time. There were consistent references to Mohammad as 'The Prophet' on the BBC. The same organization's website respectfully recited articles of the Islamic faith as straight truth, whereas Christian doctrine was, rightly, reported as a matter of claim, allegation and belief. Editorialists for whom the freedom of the Press might have been thought a bedrock value performed remarkable intellectual contortions in order to justify submission to totalitarian control of their own output.

But if the media performed shamefully, then so – tragically – did leading politicians. The most egregious response came, as has been noted before in this book, from the Foreign Secretary, Jack Straw, who apologized for the offence caused by the cartoons' publication. It was a fateful miscalculation.

In the first place, what was a Western politician doing taking responsibility for what appeared in a free media? One of the key principles that those complaining about the cartoons needed to be reminded of was that Western governments don't, can't and should not control what appears in the papers. It's no use asking the Danish government to apologize for what appears in the papers because Danish ministers, unlike those in Arab nations, do not censor, monitor and control the media.

And there's no point in firebombing Danish embassies because the people who run them don't run Danish papers.

But instead of robustly reminding the world of the nature of a free Press in a democracy, by apologizing for the cartoons Jack Straw took onto government's shoulders responsibility for the media, and in particular for the effect on Islamist opinion of what the Western Press publishes. For a government minister to apologize, in our name, for what a free Press has done is bad enough. But what is worse is the effect Mr Straw's words will have on future Islamist thinking. A precedent has now been set whereby, after a brief campaign of agitation, Islamists have managed to get Western governments to accept their test of what is and is not acceptable free expression. Islamists have tested the willingness both of our media and of our elected representatives to defend our values, our culture and our freedoms: above the acrid smoke of burning flags, they have smelt our fear.

9

Fellow Travellers

The Islamist advance has been facilitated by a variety of factors. The corruption and backwardness of most Arab and Islamic political leaders. The willingness of many in the West to support those leaders. The weakness of the West in the face of terrorism. The irresolution of the West when confronted with any difficult and lengthy conflict. The sapping of confidence in Western values encouraged by the radical Left since 1968. The failure to appreciate the scale and nature of the ideological challenge we face. The failure to stand with the nation, Israel, which has been in the front line of the struggle against Islamism. The prevailing moral relativism that has prevented a defence of our culture being mounted with the necessary self-confidence and vigour. The failure of the British state to recognize the threat posed by the most flagrant Islamists. And the continuing failure of the British state to develop the correct policy for combating extremist influences in our own country.

Each of these failures, misjudgements or errors has helped Islamism make progress. Each has weakened our culture's defences in the ongoing war against the West. But none was a conscious manoeuvre specifically designed to facilitate Islamism's advance. Yet there have been individuals and groups, apparently outside Islamist circles, who have deliberately acted in such a way as to help Islamism advance.

Perhaps the most obvious such figure in British politics is the Mayor of London, Ken Livingstone. Mr Livingstone has a long record of indulging, and supporting, terrorist causes, having been one of the first Labour politicians to champion Irish republicanism, inviting Sinn Fein leaders to Westminster while the IRA was still pursuing its military campaign.

Mr Livingstone has an unhappy habit of bringing Nazi references into his public discourse, alleging at one point that global capitalism had killed more people than Hitler ever had and, most recently, accusing a Jewish reporter of behaving like a Nazi war criminal and a concentration camp guard.[40] People who relativize the Holocaust, accuse Jews of acting like Nazis and try to characterize global capitalists as murderers are often drawn to criticism of Israel, and Mr Livingstone has been vigorous in that regard.

So perhaps it was no surprise that he should have been happy to play host to Sheikh Yusuf al-Qaradawi when the spiritual leader of the Muslim Brotherhood was invited here by the Muslim Association of Britain. Mr Livingstone's decision was criticized by, among others, Jewish groups, feminist groups, British Hindus and gay activists, including the Outrage! campaigner Peter Tatchell. Mr Livingstone has never much worried about the criticism he has attracted over the years from Jewish groups, but as the original practitioner of rainbow politics in the UK the London Mayor has always been careful to stay on the right side of other minority groups. It says something profound about Mr Livingstone's ideological orientation that he was prepared to put good relations with so many at risk in order to advance Sheikh Qaradawi's cause. Mr Livingstone even went so far as to issue a dossier defending the Sheikh against allegations of homophobia and extremism.

Since putting himself out to help the Muslim Brotherhood's spiritual leader, Mr Livingstone has offered the organization assistance in other ways. In February 2006, on the eve of the anti-cartoon rally organized by the MAB, the Brotherhood's British branch, Ken hosted a Press conference for several key Muslim Brotherhood activists. As well as Anas al-Tikriti, the former President of the Muslim Association of Britain, there was Intissar Khreeji, from the Federation of Student Islamic Societies (FOSIS), Habibur Rahman, of the Islamic Forum Europe, which played host to the Muslim Brotherhood's spiritual leader, Sheikh Qaradawi, when he visited the UK, and Dr Daud Abdullah, author of a 'tribute lecture for Hamas's guru, Shaykh Ahmad Yassin', entitled 'Not in vain, O Shaykh Yassin'.

What calculation lies behind Mr Livingstone's conspicuous embrace of Islamism? Does he believe that the electoral arithmetic in the future, especially in London, is especially favourable to those who are seen to support not just 'Islamic' causes but specifically Islamist organizations?

Most conspicuously, and notoriously, of course, the former Labour MP George Galloway defeated the Labour MP Oona King in Bethnal Green and Bow after a campaign in which Ms King's Jewish birth, her gender and her support for the liberation of Iraq were all highlighted.

Whether or not British politicians deliberately set out to pursue votes by endorsing Islamist positions, the perception that they have benefited electorally from being on that 'side' of the debate nevertheless has a worrying effect on our politics. It encourages Islamist organizations to step up their targeting of other candidates. It discourages those politicians who might otherwise speak out against Islamism from doing so, lest they attract similar attention. And it encourages ambitious politicians, and parties, to believe that one of the ways to secure political advantage in multi-ethnic Britain is to seek the favour of the most aggressive, and organized, sectional lobbies. Overall, the conclusion that Islamists will draw is, once again, one of terminal weakness. As they push, so we crumble.

But there may well be another reason why Mr Livingstone, and others like him, find themselves championing Islamist positions. It could be a matter of developing ideological alignment. A question of conviction.

As has been discussed, the development of radical thinking since 1968 has increasingly taken those on the left away from traditional economic territory and onto cultural ground. The Left's victims and heroes are no longer proletarians but guerrilla fighters in the developing world. The Left's enemies are no longer primarily a system, capitalism, and its agents, such as big business. Instead the principal enemy is now the oppressive West and, in particular, the Great Satan, America, and the Little Satan, Israel. The Crusaders and the Zionists.

For those reasons, and many others, antipathy towards America, like opposition to Israel, has become the touchstone of radical left credibility. To be anti-American, like being anti-Israel, is to be on the right side of the key struggle of our times. And so, for many on the left, all those who rise in opposition to America, and to Israel, are potential, even natural allies. And for the most committed figures on the radical spectrum those forces that are the most passionately anti-American make especially seductive partners.

That helps explain why the impeccably Trotskyist Socialist Workers' Party, Britain's oldest continuous revolutionary movement, was prepared to subsume its identity within a new political party, Respect, by fusing with the Muslim Association of Britain. That coalition has required considerable sacrifices on the part of SWP members, beyond even seeing their new party leader, George Galloway, impersonate a hungry kitten in *Celebrity Big Brother*. The SWP has had to accept positions on issues from homosexuality to abortion, and other key social questions, dictated by Islamist sensibilities.

The fusion between Islamism and the Left was given a significant boost by the campaign against the Gulf War. Just as campaigning in favour of Britain's EU membership in the 1975 referendum suggested to David Steel and Roy Jenkins that there was more that united than divided them, so working together in the circumstances of the Stop The War campaign allowed totalitarians of the left, like the SWP's John Rees and Lindsey German, to discover the common ground they shared with Islamist totalitarians. The sense of commonality between them is signified by more than the shared platform on which they stood in the 2005 election. It was telling that Respect felt the need to brief the Press that its leading activist Lindsey German was not the same person as the 7/7 bomber Jermaine Lindsay.

There are, however, some genuinely intriguing figures in the ranks of Respect. The party's biggest funder, Dr Mohammad Naseem, chairman of Birmingham Central Mosque, is also leader of the Islamic Party of Britain, which supports the death penalty for homosexuality. Dr Naseem's party takes an individual line on other matters. It has argued that the 7/7 attacks were a provocation, staged by the police, the Blair government, or Mossad. When the videotape emerged in which Mohammad Siddique Khan took responsibility for the attack, Dr Naseem argued that it could have been doctored. He said: 'We are in the twenty-first century. The cows can be made to look as dancing, the horses can speak like humans, so these things can be doctored or can be produced.'[41]

One of Dr Naseem's close colleagues was the Birmingham Sparkbrook and Small Heath candidate in the 2005 election, Salma Yaqoob, who has also acted as a spokesperson for the mosque. That is not the only organization she has spoken up for. Ms Yaqoob also acted as Press Officer for the Justice for Britons in Yemen campaign, a group that campaigned on behalf of those British jihadists sent to Yemen by Sheikh Abu Hamza.

It is not just within the membership of Respect that the ties that bind the radical Left and radical Islam can be discerned. The Comment pages of the *Guardian* newspaper regularly allow Islamist sympathizers to rub shoulders with advocates of SWP positions. So Anas al-Tikriti and Seumas Milne, Azzam al-Tamimi and Louise Christian form a United Front against America and Israel.

This openness to Islamism has, on occasions, embarrassed even the *Guardian*'s editors. Five days after the 7/7 bombings one of the *Guardian*'s own trainees, Dilpazier Islam, was commissioned to write a piece entitled 'We rock the boat: today's Muslims aren't prepared to ignore injustice'. It was subsequently revealed that Mr Islam was a member of the Islamist group Hizb ut-Tehrir, and when some of HuT's past comments and positions were brought to light the *Guardian* was compelled to part company with him.[42] The *Guardian* was clearly uncomfortable with the situation and offered its readers a full explanation of the matter at the end of July 2005. But Mr Islam could be forgiven for wondering just what in HuT's Islamist outlook is beyond the pale when Muslim Brotherhood activists such as Azzam al-Tamimi still grace the *Guardian*'s pages.

The coincidence of values, interests and outlook between so many on the radical left and Islamists is still under-appreciated, and under-explored, partly because of the broader denial in which too many engage about the scale of the problem we face. If only, they argue, we stay out of foreign wars and shield our eyes from alien struggles, then we will avoid drawing attention to ourselves, and thus avoid endangering our people. It is a seductive thought. But tragically misconceived.

10

A Challenge That Cannot Be Ducked

In the aftermath of 7/7 the predominant media and political consensus on causation was brutally direct. This was 'blow-back' from Iraq. We had been warned that going to war in the Gulf would expose us to further terrorist attack; and here was the grim evidence. We had bombed Baghdad. Now the bombs were exploding on our streets.

So determined was the media establishment to make this charge stick that it marginalized almost every other analysis or investigation into the wellsprings of Islamist violence. Instead, the chief duty of journalists became trying to trip Tony Blair, or one of his ministers, into 'admitting' the linkage. Instead of serving the public interest, the media, in particular the public service broadcasters, kept up an interminable game of 'Gotcha!'

If indeed there was a direct linkage between the Iraq War and 7/7, then one would have thought that those responsible for the bombing would have used their posthumous videotape to make that causal link explicit. But Mohammad Siddique Khan refrained from singling out Iraq as the spark that lit the fuse. Even if Khan failed to make that linkage, one might expect, if Iraq was a causal factor in the radicalization of Muslim opinion, that this would show up in objective tests of Muslim feeling.

But a study of the polling data conducted by Garvan Walshe shows no direct causal link between the Iraq intervention in 2003 and a shift in Muslim attitudes. If one looks at the direct relationship between the Iraq War and a willingness among Muslims to support violence against the West there seems to be no drive to 'retaliation' as a consequence of intervention. According to ICM polls the proportion of Muslims supporting either September 11th or 'al Qaeda or similar organizations' attacking the United States was 15 per cent in 2001, 11 per cent in 2002 and 13 per cent in 2004.

It is certainly the case that the war in Iraq was unpopular with many Muslims in the West. Although not all, as anyone with Kurdish friends will be aware. But then so was the intervention in Afghanistan. In a March 2004 ICM poll of British Muslims, 80 per cent thought the Iraq War was unjustified. But in an ICM poll carried out in November 2001, 80 per cent of British Muslims thought the war in Afghanistan was unjustified.

The intervention in Afghanistan certainly enjoyed more support among the media and political classes than the war in Iraq. While the former was viewed by a sufficient number as legitimate self-defence, the latter was almost universally derided as dangerous adventurism. There may therefore have been an assumption that what drove John Humphrys to distraction should have had an even more incendiary effect on Britain's young Muslims. But the opinion data suggest that, far from marking a uniquely radicalizing moment for British Muslims, the war in Iraq was simply another one of a series of interventions with which a majority disagreed.

Radical left-wingers such as John Pilger,[43] and traditional right-wingers such as Correlli Barnett,[44] nevertheless argue that, given the general level of Muslim discontent with Western foreign policy, we should abandon intervention altogether, so as not to antagonize Islamic opinion. It is worth while to ask whether it would ever be right for a democracy to give veto power over its foreign policy to any particular minority, but it is particularly worth while to reflect on the wisdom of allowing a specific religious minority's sensibilities to dictate a country's relations with the rest of the world. And, in any case, how could we be sure which foreign policy postures we adopted were and which were not provocative to radical Muslim or Islamist opinion? Indeed, even if we pursued a foreign policy as timorous as Liechtenstein's, what is to prevent a domestic turn of events antagonizing Islamist critics? What if our courts were to rule against a particular form of religious dress, or our publishers to allow a particular libel to be disseminated about Mohammad? How could we possibly insulate ourselves from Islamist anger without surrendering the freedom that makes us distinctively Western? Once we start framing our foreign policy so as not to offend Islamists, where will our accommodation with their agenda end? Once you start paying the Danegeld, you never get rid of the Dane.

The truth, as we have already seen, is that it has been weakness, timidity, irresolution and retreat in the face of Islamist aggression that has most encouraged terrorists to believe they are on the right path. But before terrorists can be encouraged to act as they do, they have to be drawn down a path that inclines them to listen. As we have seen, much of that process of ideological priming is facilitated by the vigour and influence of Islamist thought in Britain, and across the world.

But there are specific social and political factors that can lead to marginalization, and lay individuals more open to the totalitarian temptation. There are specific trends at work in British society that may well open the way to encouraging some young Muslim men towards greater radicalism.

As already noted, there has been a pernicious tendency in British state practice to privilege the specifically Islamic identity of young Muslims over other allegiances. The Cantle report, commissioned by the government after disturbances in Pennine towns, warned that the structure of state support within those communities worked against social cohesion. Over the years community leaders have sought financial support for organizations that operated to a specifically Islamic agenda. It was through Islamic centres, Islamic charities, Islamic-run voluntary groups that largesse was dispensed, entrenching a sense of separateness. More than that, the need to foster, and assert, grievances was seen as the route to securing additional state support. Encouraging a belief in the existence of specifically 'anti-Muslim' feeling was the way to secure compensation and aid.

While it is undeniable, and indeed a source of shame, that racism and discrimination still exist across Britain, in a way that manifestly hits Britons from a South Asian background, it has been in the interests of certain community leaders and organizations to turn this into a specifically anti-Muslim narrative. In so doing they have fed a feeling of alienation and grievance that pits Muslims against the rest of society, not just in a competition to see who can most effectively claim victim status, but in the broader sense of reinforcing a perception of 'internal exile'.

The Cantle report also found that the teaching, and understanding, of English was not encouraged as it should have been. Not least because some community leaders owed their status to their ability to act as intermediaries between the state and minority groups. The broader participation that a more widespread use of English might bring about would, in their eyes, have potentially undermined their authority.

Social and family patterns can also play a part in reinforcing this process of marginalization. There is a greater than average tendency among British Muslims from South Asian backgrounds to marry spouses from the subcontinent. Other ethnic minority groups are more likely to marry out, or form partnerships with others from the same background who have lived all their lives in Britain. This trend among South Asian Muslims can mean that the family space is less 'Westernized' than within other ethnic minority groups. The habits, mores, sexual relations and cultural assumptions within such households are likely to be more traditional, and distant from the rest of contemporary British society.

All these factors may feed a sense of separateness, as may others, including relative economic deprivation. Even among those Muslims who are economically more successful, or more visibly integrated into the patterns of the rest of British life, there may be a sense of guilt at 'leaving behind' traditional patterns of life in order to succeed on Western terms.

Radical Islam and its advocates have become adept at playing on these feelings of separation, alienation and anxiety. Islamists will tell their listeners that yes, they are different. And so they should be. Islam sets them apart. They are possessors of a superior revelation that places them not just at a distance from, but above, the rest of British society. Western society is antagonistic to Islam, as all rotten and decadent societies are antagonistic to movements that threaten their assumptions. And that is why Muslims suffer prejudice, or discrimination. It is because the West is trying to put them down, along with their faith. Muslim uncertainties and anxieties spring from attempts to live by Western rules, which are not just rigged against them, but harmful to the soul.

I had the privilege of seeing just such arguments made by

Islamists to an audience of British Muslims when I accepted an invitation to join a 'discussion panel' established by a Muslim professional anxious to 'encourage dialogue'. The gentleman concerned, a West London doctor, was a charming and persuasive soul.[45] He was also an activist with Hizb ut-Tehrir, and it became clear to me as the afternoon went on that my role on the panel (as a supporter of Israel, feminism, gay rights and President Bush) was to display the true horror of modern secular Britain. My co-panellists were all passionate Islamists, and the appeal made by the Hizb ut-Tehrir speaker in particular was brilliantly pitched to encourage disgust with the West and pride in Islam of the most theologically conservative and politically radical kind.

What was particularly striking was how little foreign affairs entered into his, and his colleagues', pitch. It was not the West's actions abroad that inspired his most passionate denunciations, but the nature of the West itself. Our sexual licence, our system of commerce, our rejection of revealed established faith in favour of shallow personal exploration, the shamelessness of young women, the empty, drug-fuelled, football-mad hedonism of young men. The litany was intended to fuel not just disgust with the West, but also feelings of self-disgust at the memory of temptations felt, and perhaps indulged. The call being issued was for purity, and purification, personal internal reform and external political change, the lesser and the greater jihad.

What is to Be Done

T he war against the West that I have described is being fought on many levels. In that respect it follows the pattern of the Cold War struggle against communism.

There is a global dimension, as Islamists and their allies try to secure geopolitical advantage by winning territory, co-opting governments, subverting states that seem ripe for overwhelming, and testing the enemy's resolution through direct combat.

There is a specific national dimension, here in the UK and in other Western states, as Islamist ideologues, like communists before them, seek to capture organizations, establish front movements, recruit the impressionable young, drive the media agenda and throw governments off balance.

There is also an ideological, even intellectual, bridge between the two as Islamists seek to win a broader battle of ideas, appealing to Muslims everywhere to throw off the shackles of *jahiliyya*, escape the barbarism in which they are sunk, and bring forward the millenarian dream of a world reborn. A vital complement to that battle is the need to undermine, further weaken and eventually overcome Western resistance to Islamism's march. Given that the West is not just a barrier to Islamism's advance, but its antithesis, the battle is urgent and central.

There are, of course, many differences between the threat we faced from communist totalitarianism and the challenge posed by Islamism. There are no Islamic armoured divisions ready to strike through the Fulda Gap at a moment's notice. Instead we face a daily threat of terrorist violence from an enemy prepared to strike without notice or warning, to slaughter without limit.

Given the scale of the challenge we face, the response required has to be similarly broad, thoughtful and, above all, resilient. That applies particularly to the global and geopolitical steps we need to take. This book has been written in the lengthening shadow cast by the conflict in Iraq, and the difficulties the coalition has encountered there have only increased the level of opposition towards the idea of a forward Western policy in the war against terror.

Much ink has been spilt on the wisdom, or otherwise, of the path that George W. Bush and Tony Blair took. Ultimately, as the Prime Minister has pointed out, the judgement on their decision-making will rest with posterity and the Almighty. But despite all that has been written about Iraq, much still needs saying.

In judging any human action, before one condemns what has been done it is wise to ask what the consequences of inaction would have been. What would have happened if the coalition had not taken action against Saddam Hussein?

On the most basic level, a murderous tyrant would still have been in power, using torture as an instrument of policy and a tool of amusement, presiding over an apparatus of oppression that killed more of his fellow citizens every year than have been claimed by all the tragedies since liberation. Saddam would have been looking forward to bequeathing intact his regime, and its oil wealth, to one of his sons, either Uday or Qusay. From what we know of both they would have made their father seem a model of restraint.

If Saddam were still in place now, then we can be sure that the UN sanctions applied against him would not be. Those restraints, imperfect and corruptly administered as they were, still prevented him from equipping his war machine as he wished. But those sanctions were fraying before the Gulf War. Given how France and Germany had been eager to trade with Saddam in the past, and bearing in mind the attitude of Russia and China to trading with rogue states, from Venezuela through Sudan to Iran, we can be certain that if sanctions had survived, they would be in name only.

So, a Saddam left free to terrorize his own people, free to pass on his regime to his psychopath sons, free to trade, free to arm; and a Saddam who would, if he had survived in power to this day, have only reinforced his position as living proof that the West could be defied and there was no price to pay. We know that Saddam's survival after the First Gulf War encouraged and inspired anti-Western forces everywhere. How would they have reacted if he had been allowed to maintain his posture of defiance against the West indefinitely, and unmolested? If America could not deal with Saddam, the tyrant who had faced the Great Satan's forces in 1991, who had outwitted its arms' inspectors, who thumbed his nose at the international order, who plotted the assassination of US presidents, who rejoiced at 9/11 and dreamed of emulating it, then who could it deal with?

More than that, a Saddam still in power, with sanctions a dead letter, would undeniably have been determined to pursue both his WMD programme and his links with terrorism. We know now that Saddam had already invited jihadists into Iraq to join him in his fight against the West. Some of them are fighting us now. And we know that he had never abandoned the dream of acquiring nuclear weaponry, for the prestige it would give him, for the potential havoc it could wreak, and as a means of self-defence against a similarly armed Iran.

For all those reasons, inaction would have brought massive risks. Risks that most are inclined to ignore or discount in their desire to bash Bush, blast Blair and knock the West.

Of course, Bush and Blair have made mistakes. No conflict has ever unfolded with all the choreographed perfection of a theatre performance. And some of those mistakes have been grievous. But many of the mistakes laid at their door constitute entirely the wrong critique.

Yes, it is true that the coalition lacked a sufficiently comprehensive plan for all eventualities. And yes, it is powerfully true that the coalition has, throughout, had too few troops in Iraq. So far, so conventional, so true.

But the other criticisms ritually made – the folly of disbanding the Iraqi army, the over-zealous de-Ba'athification process, the heavy-handedness of military intervention by the Americans – are less sustainable.

Much of the existing army disbanded itself. And, in any case, its existing structures could not be relied on in a new Iraq. De-Ba'athification, the removal of Saddam's party loyalists from positions of influence, was a necessary prelude to establishing faith in any new Iraqi government. Indeed for most Iraqis it did not go far enough. The lingering presence of so many ex-Ba'athists in positions of power only fed suspicions that too little had changed.

The reason why de-Ba'athification didn't actually go further sprang from British Foreign Office fears that too vigorous a purge would necessarily mean Sunni under-representation, and that would alienate Britain's traditional Sunni allies in Saudi Arabia and the Gulf. In the process, however, we succeeded only in testing the patience and loyalty of the Shia majority as well as genuine Sunni democrats.

The allegations made against the US military of excessive force crucially misunderstand what was required, and what is still required, in Iraq. The insurgency in Iraq is made up of ex-Ba'athists and jihadists, both indigenous and foreign. Together they have become an effectively Islamist-led alliance. And they have been trying to recreate in central Iraq what they once enjoyed in Afghanistan, an Islamist-run space in which terrorists can be trained and blooded, and from which future jihadi activity can be launched.

It is hugely important for the West to defeat the insurgency, and in the process to deliver a critical blow against Islamism. That means the terrorists must be denied space, see their operations overwhelmed consistently by superior force, and be faced with an enemy growing in strength and confidence even as it meets with frustration and loss. In that respect the intention behind the action in Fallujah made perfect sense. What has tragically undermined the coalition has been a lack of resources.

All the current talk of withdrawing allied forces, as Iraqi troop numbers grow, misses the point. When fighting a war, one wants to win, as quickly and effectively as possible. That means concentrating strength, not dissipating it. As Senator John McCain has wisely pointed out, we are in Iraq to fight terror, so as the Iraqis stand up we shouldn't stand down, we should use their strength to augment our own in engaging with the jihadists. To retreat now, which is what is contemplated, will not only weaken the ability of the Iraqi state to deal with the insurgency; it will, in the most important front we have in the War on Terror, fatally signal our own lack of stomach for the long haul.

The reason the jihadists fight with such vigour in Iraq is that they already sense the lack of Western resolution. British forces in the south, praised in the past for the restraint with which they policed their areas of responsibility, are now increasingly restricted to barracks. Their primary mission now is simply self-preservation. Their current posture does not stem from any lack of resolution or bravery on the part of the military, but again is related to the Foreign Office view that governed the initial deployment. For the FCO, at that point fully committed to a programme of constructive engagement with Iran, the imperative in the Shia south was effectively to appease Iranian interests. So ground was ceded to Iranian-backed militias, and with that ground, authority. The consequences of this policy were doubly hazardous. Not only was a lack of resolution communicated to radicals and extremists, but opportunities were created for Iranian-backed forces to acquire the space and weaponry to more effectively target British forces on the ground.

Throughout our time in Iraq our mission has been compromised by a lack of clear and decisive thinking. Western diplomatic establishments have tried to buy the compliance of neighbouring regimes such as Saudi Arabia and Iran by shaping Iraqi policy to fit their concerns. This approach has only disheartened Iraqi democrats and encouraged the jihadists, whose low estimation of our willingness to shoulder the required burden is in the process of being confirmed.

Our ability to follow the appropriate policy has, in any case, been compromised by our inability to commit the levels of troops required not just to signal seriousness of intent but to get the job done. For that, and that chiefly, George W. Bush and Tony Blair deserve to be criticized.

But that criticism must always be placed in context. Worrying as the failures have been in Iraq, and ominous as the trumpeted plans for withdrawal must seem, there have been achievements worth recording in Iraq, beyond the basic imperative to rid the world of a tyrant whose continuance in office would have left us unable, credibly, to act anywhere else.

The greatest of these has been the advance of democratic values in the Arab world, a cause noble in itself and vital in the greater struggle we face. The millions of Iraqis who defied terrorist violence and shamed Western cynics to turn out and vote in the country's elections and referendum reaffirmed the precious universality of human rights. Their enthusiasm for democracy, and the potential for change, growth and freedom that it offers, was inspiring. What was sobering was the knowledge that the only free and fair elections that have ever occurred in Arab nations have been in territories under occupation.

Before, and since, the elections in December 2005, the people of Iraq have had to endure a ferocious terrorist onslaught, an assault, as we have seen, from which we have not done enough to protect them. The savagery of the assault is driven by one overwhelming imperative. The jihadists behind it recognize that if democracy does take root in Iraq, and then spread, their room for advance will be decisively checked. In a letter written by Abu Musab al-Zarqawi in 2004, the Al Qaeda commander in Iraq in 2004 explains to his followers the decisive threat to their project posed by the establishment and spread of democracy. He also makes clear what his counter-strategy will be:

> Fighting the Shi'a is the way to take the nation to battle. The Shi'a have taken on the dress of the army, police and the Iraqi security forces, and have raised the banner of protecting the nation, and the citizens.

Since the Zarqawi letter was intercepted it has been clear that the jihadists are following precisely that path. The relentless targeting of Shia civilians, Shia holy sites, is intended to trigger retaliation and escalation. The stoicism of the vast majority of Shias, and of Ayatollah Ali Sistani, under such sustained assault, is humbling. They deserve even more sustained support than they have yet received, not just because their stand has been a noble one, but also because the endurance of democracy in Iraq is vital for the region. Should Iraq's infant democracy collapse then it would be the biggest single victory the Islamists have had, or could conceive of, in our lifetime.

As it is, the establishment of democracy in Iraq has already had a welcome effect on the wider Middle East. It is now almost impossible to talk to any figure in the Arab world, or the Gulf, without them having to concede the vital importance of 'reform'. And while that word may mean no more than technocratic change for some leaders, others are feeling the wind at their back. Several of the Gulf states have had to move towards a greater degree of public consultation in their governance. Even Saudi Arabia and Egypt have felt sufficiently under pressure to hold their own, sadly staged and compromised, exercises in quasi-democracy.

Much more importantly, however, there have been signs of people power asserting itself across the Middle East. In Iran students and bus-drivers have been among the groups determined to take the fight against the Islamist establishment on to the streets. And in Lebanon open public protest has forced Syria to withdraw its forces, and give that nation room to breathe again. Even though Damascus still retains a significant, and malign, influence over Lebanon, the Lebanese are well on their way to regaining their freedom. And as the Druze leader Walid Jumblatt, no friend of the West, has made clear, none of this would have been possible without the liberation of Iraq.

The ultimate importance of the spread of democracy in the Middle East is hard to overstate. In the first place it is a matter of simple, and prudent, statecraft. If Iran were a proper democracy, with its leaders answerable to its people and compelled, as democratic governments are, to put their welfare first, then it would be unlikely to be pursuing a nuclear weapons programme. And even if it were, then we would have no more need, intrinsically, to worry than we have because France or India have nuclear weapons because they are democracies. As Natan Sharansky has pointed out in his brilliant book *The Case for Democracy*, nations that enjoy proper representative government, and the freedoms it brings, do not prejudice those freedoms and their people's interests by pursuing policies of terror against their neighbours. The iron rule of history is that tyrannies begin by making war on their own people and end by making war on everyone else. If we wish to live in a more peaceful world we should want it to be more democratic.

The second reason why the spread of democracy is particularly vital in the Middle East is that it is the best solvent yet devised for Islamism. Those nations that have tried to suppress Islamism by remaining tyrannies themselves, such as Saudi Arabia, Syria and Egypt, have ended up either paying Islamists off, subsidizing their work abroad, or watching impotently as the Islamists continue their advance. As we have seen across the Middle East, from Palestine to Riyadh, Islamists have exploited the backwardness, corruption and cynicism of past generations of Arab leaders to make themselves the principal, and apparently principled, opposition. Since no Arab nation currently allows a flourishing secular space for opposition to grow, there is nowhere else to go for those who wish to protest other than underground, and into the arms of the Islamists. Given the massive and spectacular corruption of the Saudis and the House of Mubarak, it is perhaps a wonder that more are not tempted by the Islamist promise.

There is a third, and related, reason why the spread of

democracy is important in itself. The people of the Arab
Middle East deserve a better life. After years of betrayal, mis-
government and oppression, the Arab people deserve the
opportunity to enjoy the same rights and freedoms that we
have in the West. Inevitably, Arab democracies will have a
different character from those in the West, just as Japan is dif-
ferently constituted from Germany. But if both those countries
can make the transition from fascism to democracy in a generation, then why can't others, which have lived through far lesser traumas?

The Islamists are, in that respect, right that the West is their
mortal enemy, and we shouldn't be ashamed to say so. If we
believe in the superiority of our way of life, if we believe, as the
anti-apartheid movement and the civil rights movement
believed, that freedom knows no boundaries and every human
being is precious, then we should believe in, and want urgently
to work for, the spread of democracy across the globe.

But standing up for our values abroad is only one half of
the struggle we have to engage in. There is also an urgent need
to defend them at home.

That will require changes in the way our security and justice systems operate. The demands of national security are
different from those of criminal justice, and governments
have traditionally accepted the need for exceptional legislation and the temporary curtailment of liberties. We should be
clear that these are needed again. But clearer still that they
must be temporary.

We cannot be serious about defending liberty unless we
ensure, through proper parliamentary accountability, that legislation designed to deal with a specific terrorist threat is on the
Statute Book for only as long as the threat exists. But we also
cannot be taken seriously when we try to defend democracy
unless we ensure that we show resolution in framing the laws
necessary to prevent terrorists operating freely.

There are specific changes to the way in which our law operates that do need to be seriously considered. Not least the mess in which our courts now find themselves as a result of this government's application of the Human Rights Act.

Consider just two cases. In 2002, the High Court rejected the extradition of the Algerian Rachid Ramda to France, even though Ramda was wanted in connection with allegations of financing a series of bombings.[46] Simply because the court feared that the evidence against Ramda had come from a co-accused who it was alleged had suffered ill-treatment at the hands of the French.

The man believed to be the head of the Moroccan Islamic Combatant Group, the organization behind terrorist bombings in Madrid and Casablanca, Mohammad al-Guerbuzi, was sentenced to 20 years in prison in Morocco in December 2003. But Mr al-Guerbuzi is currently living in London, where he has been allowed to remain at liberty for years. Requests from both Spain and Morocco to extradite him have been rejected.

The problems we face are compounded by the dogged refusal of too many in the legal establishment to put the defence of our civilization ahead of the defence of the traditions with which their profession has grown comfortable.

When a senior Law Lord such as Leonard Hoffmann can say of attempts to restrain the liberty of Islamist ideologues that 'the real threat to the life of the nation comes not from terrorism but from laws such as these', then we know we are living in a land that has still not woken up to the challenge we face.

Changing our laws, vital as it is, can only, however, be one part of our response. We need to display resolution in the way we pay for our security, ensuring that our intelligence services and armed services are funded properly. We also need to ensure that they get the political leadership they deserve to tackle the problems we face. That means a leadership prepared to recognize the essential link between the display of weakness in the past and the Islamist advance we face today.

More broadly, we also need to rediscover and reproclaim faith in our common values. We need an ideological effort to move away from moral relativism and towards moral clarity, as well as a commitment to build a truly inclusive model of British citizenship in which divisive separatist identities are challenged, and rejected.

If we choose this path sensitivities will be offended, special interests upset and powerful voices raised in opposition. But unless we show that we are serious about defeating the forces that have encouraged Islamist terrorism, then Islamist terrorists will have many opportunities in the future to prove just how serious they are about using force to defeat us.

Notes

1   BBC TV, *Newsnight*, 3 February 2006
2   *Guardian*, 18 February 1989
3   *New Humanist*, 1 June 2002
4   Foreign and Commonwealth Office press conference, 3 February 2006
5   'Bosnia Report', January-March 2004 (Bosnian Institute)
6   BBC News, 9 June 2005
7   Intelligence and Terrorism Information Center at the Center for Special Studies
8   BBC News, 14 December 2005
9   'Holocaust!? Again', Mohammad Daoud, *Syria Times*, 6 September 2000
10 'Likely PA Prime Minister a Holocaust-Denier', Rafael Medoff, 26 February 2003
11 BBC News, 1 January 2001
12 BBC News 1 July 2003
13 'Radical Chic and Mau-Mauing the Flak Catchers', Tom Wolfe, 1970
14 BBC News, 12 August 2005

15 Aljazeera, 12 August 2005
16 BBC News, 27 July 2005
17 BBC News, 27 July 2005
18 BBC News, 12 August 2005
19 'The Portal for Britain's Suicide Terrorists', Michael Whine, Al-Muhajiroun, 21 May 2003
20 *Daily Telegraph*, 27 April 2004
21 *Daily Telegraph*, 29 November 2005
22 Whine, ibid
23 BBC News, 12 August 2005
24 BBC News, 3 February 2003
25 BBC News, 3 February 2003
26 *Daily Mail*, 11 February 2006
27 'The Lawful and the Prohibited in Islam', Yusuf al-Quaradwi (Kuwait: International Federation of Student Organization, 1984)
28 *Daily Mail*, 11 February 2006
29 *Guardian*, 18 February 1989
30 BBC News, 14 July 2005
31 *Daily Telegraph*, 21 August 2005
32 *Daily Telegraph,* 21 August 2005
33 *Observer,* 26 February 2006
34 RFE/RL, 15 June 2004
35 Panorama, 21 August 2005
36 *Sunday Times*, 11 September 2005
37 'Inquiry and Analysis' (266), Middle East Media Research Institute
38 *Spectator*, 24 July 2004
39 *Daily Telegraph*, 2 March 2006
40 BBC News, 6 March 2001
41 BBC News, 3 September 2005
42 *Guardian*, 22 July 2005
43 *Mirror*, 1 November 2001
44 *Spectator*, 13 December 2003
45 *Prospect* (114), September 2005
46 *Daily Telegraph*, 1 March 2006

Acknowledgements

The inspiration for this book came from George Weidenfeld, a man of great wisdom and humanity whom I am proud to be able to call a friend. It was his idea that I should write a short work tackling head on much of the nonsense which had been spoken and written about terrorism in the last few years, and I am immensely grateful to him for the opportunity.

I am also grateful to the team at Weidenfeld & Nicolson who showed exemplary forebearance and understanding throughout the writing process. Their editing skill saved me from committing a number of schoolboy errors and their judgement enabled me to bring clarity to my thoughts. I am particularly grateful to Alan Samson and Lucinda McNeile for all their hard work and patience.

Much of the argument I make in this book has grown out of the journalism I have produced for *The Times* over the last ten years. During that period I have been helped enormously in developing my thoughts by a wonderful team of colleagues. I should like, in particular, to thank all those editors who showed faith in my work, particularly Peter Stothard, Ben Preston and Robert Thomson, as well as Daniel Finkelstein, Tim Hames and Sandra Parsons.

I am also grateful to the BBC for giving me the opportunity to appear on Radio Four's *The Moral Maze* for two years, during which time some of the issues in this book were debated. And therefore I must place on record my thanks to the programme's producer, David Coomes, its presenter Michael Buerk, and my fellow panelists, Melanie Phillips, Steven Rose, Claire Fox, Ian Hargreaves and Clifford Longley.

I also owe a considerable debt to friends and colleagues across the journalistic and political spectrum whose conversation and ideas have helped shape my thinking. I am particularly indebted to Dean Godson and Nicholas Boles of the think tank Policy Exchange, Dominic Cummings and James Frayne, formerly of the New Frontiers Foundation, Garvan Walshe and Glyn Gaskarth of the Conservative Research Department and the writers Simon Sebag Montefiore, Stephen Pollard, Oliver Kamm, William Shawcross and Douglas Murray. Several friends were kind enough to read an early draft of the argument and made many useful comments. The mistakes, of fact or judgement, which remain are entirely my own.

As a practising politician I also depend hugely on the support, and good sense, of my friends and colleagues in politics. I am therefore particularly grateful to the officers of Surrey Heath Conservative Association, especially its past Chairmen Peter Harper and Richard Robinson as well as its current Chairman, Nigel Manning and Agent, Alan Cleverly. I could not have completed this work, short as it is, without the immense hard work, patience and tact of my office colleagues Karen Sheerer and Robert Nemeth. Nor could I have developed the arguments in here without the robust testing they were given by a variety of parliamentary colleagues.

The final, and deepest, debt I owe is to my wife Sarah. It is immeasurable.

Index